# POETS

# about

# POETRY

## Interviews with Contemporary American Poets

### H. Philip Hsieh

Published by
EGW Publishing
(Since 1979)

Copyright 2016 by H. Philip Hsieh
All rights reserved
Printed in the United States of America
Cover Photograph: Yung-Chien Lew

All rights reserved. No part of this book may be reproduced or transmitted in any form, or by any means, without written permission from the author.

EGW Publishing (since 1979)

ISBN 978-0-916393-23-6

EGW Publishing
4075 Papazian Way
Suite 105
Fremont, California 94538

www.egwpublishing.com

For my wife

Meishiang Hwang Hsieh

# Contents

| | |
|---|---|
| Preface | 11 |
| Lawrence Ferlinghetti | 14 |
| Maxine Kumin | 26 |
| Jerry Ball | 34 |
| William Marr | 44 |
| Roald Hoffmann | 62 |
| Ted Kooser | 82 |
| Nikki Giovanni | 88 |
| Juan Felipe Herrera | 96 |
| Christopher Herold | 108 |
| Joy Harjo | 124 |
| Naomi Shihab Nye | 136 |
| Rita Dove | 144 |
| Jane Hirshfield | 158 |
| Li-Young Lee | 170 |
| Index | 195 |

# Preface

Over the course of five years beginning in 2008, I took on the challenge of introducing the contemporary American poetry landscape to Chinese readers in Chiu Shui Poetry Quarterly published in Taiwan. Most of the articles in my column documented my interviews of fourteen contemporary American poets. With one exception, the interviews were conducted originally in English and then translated into Chinese for the benefits of the anticipated readers. Along the way, I've been encouraged by my circle of friends who enjoy poetry in English, especially in Jerry Ball's Tuesday poetry class, to publish the interviews in their original language.

Special care was given that the interview questions explore fresh aspects and insights of the poets' viewpoints on poetry. Attempts were made not to repeat the same questions that had often been asked.

I could never express enough gratitude to all those fourteen renowned poets with a diversity of backgrounds for their permissions to have the original interviews printed in English for this book.

Thanks to EGW Publishing Inc., those stimulating interviews are now organized into a single volume easy for reference. While the majority of the interviews were conducted by emails for the convenience of the poets, some took the form of face-to-face chats, telephone conversations or correspondences. To make up for the lack of immediate spontaneity in the cases of correspondences and emails, a series of exchanges were made after the first contact to make the interviews complete.

I am deeply indebted to Jerry Ball, Wayne Lin and Christine Horner for their constant encouragement. Christine's much appreciated constructive and specific comments have helped shape this book to its present form.

I would also like to acknowledge the elegant front cover photograph taken by Yung-Chien Lew, RCA (Royal Canadian Academy of Arts) and the meticulous editing help provided by Chris Slaughter at EGW Publishing, Inc.

# Lawrence Ferlinghetti

(Credit: Stacey Lewis)

Born in Yonkers, New York in 1919, Lawrence Ferlinghetti was one of the two founders of the famous bookstore, publishing house and San Francisco landmark, City Lights Booksellers and Publishers in 1953. It has been a vanguard of the alternative voices in America today since the days of the Beat generation. City Lights' publication of the then controversial poetry book *Howl* by Allen Ginsberg drew national attention during the trial on obscenity charges.

In his own right, Ferlinghetti is a very well established poet and painter. His enthusiasm in poetry and anti-war stance has earned him much respect in the circle of literature and arts.

Ferlinghetti has published numerous books on poetry, prose, novels and plays. Among his poetry collections are classics such as *A Coney Island of the Mind, Pictures of the Gone World* and *Poetry as Insurgent Art*. He has received numerous awards, including the Robert Frost Memorial Medal, the Author's Guild Lifetime Achievement Award and the National Book Critics Circle Award.

The interview was conducted by telephone on May 27, 2009.

*Philip Hsieh*: First I'd like to say thank you so much for agreeing to this interview.

*Lawrence Ferlinghetti*: What's the magazine do you write the column for?

*Hsieh*: It's called *Chiu Shui Poetry Quarterly*. Chiu Shui in Chinese means autumn water.

*Ferlinghetti*: Where is that magazine published?

*Hsieh*: It's published in Taiwan, but circulated among Chinese readers all over the world including the U.S. and China.

*Ferlinghetti*: Is it in print or online?

*Hsieh*: It's in print. I've heard your name for a long time. It's an honor for me to do the interview. First question: Why did you start a one-of-a-kind bookstore such as City Lights?

*Ferlinghetti*: Why not?

*Hsieh*: What did you envision the bookstore would be when you started City Lights? What kinds of needs did you see that City Lights filled that other bookstores didn't?

*Ferlinghetti*: When I arrived in SF in 1950, the old fashioned bookstores weren't open at night and they were closed on the weekends. And they had no places to sit down and read. Usually the clerk was on top of you right away, wanting to know what you wanted.

There were no periodicals, no magazines or newspapers in the stores. Right from the beginning we opened 7 days a week past midnight. Our first manager was Shigeyoshi Murao. He's a Japanese American. He's a chess player and liked to stay up all night. He kept the bookstore open until 2 AM. Now we are open 'til midnight, seven days a week. From the beginning, we had a big periodical section. We had newspapers and magazines that were hard to find on most newsstands. From the beginning we had magazines from the furthest left to the furthest right. We had the first lesbian and gay magazines. Those days it was very unusual for a bookstore to have that kind of thing. Today you don't realize it because now every bookstore has them.

*Hsieh*: City Lights was also the first to publish paperbacks exclusively. Isn't it?

*Ferlinghetti*: We were the first paperback bookstore. There were paper pocket books. They were all mass-market paperbacks: murder mysteries and thrillers and sex books. No quality paperbacks. No quality literature. We started even before big New York publishers started publishing paperbacks. Doubleday started the Anchor books after we did. Knopf had a line of paperbacks after us. But of course our publication was limited. We were a small bookstore and publisher. Another thing from the beginning of the bookstore was that we tried to be a community center. That's why we are still surviving and so many others have gone broke today.

*Hsieh*: Yes, particularly the independent bookstores.

*Ferlinghetti*: Yes. We have always been a community center. One of our early slogans was "the literary meeting place since 1953". That was the whole vision of the bookstore. And we also made it look like a café even though we didn't serve coffee because coffee and books don't mix very well.

*Hsieh*: Ya. I understand.

*Ferlinghetti*: So we looked like a café. We had round café tables to sit and read.

*Hsieh*: I've been to the City Lights a few times. I remembered there was a sign saying that this was like a library or something to that effect.

*Ferlinghetti*: Oh, ya. "This is a kind of library where books are sold."

*Hsieh*: Right.

*Ferlinghetti*: I put up a new line a couple of months ago. It's "a literary habitat."

*Hsieh*: Yes. Yes. Isn't it on your website *www.citylights.com*?

*Ferlinghetti*: Ya. "Literary habitat for humanity," which I'm taking off of President Carter's Habitat for Humanity project.

*Hsieh*: That sounds pretty cool. When you published Allen Ginsberg's *Howl*, did you expect to draw such a national and international attention?

*Ferlinghetti*: Well, we hoped so.

*Hsieh*: So that was part of the plan?

*Ferlinghetti*: I figured we would be busted for it. So I took the manuscript to the ACLU before it went to the printer. I said if we got arrested for publishing this, would you defend us and ACLU committed themselves ahead of time to defend us. So we weren't exactly flying blind.

*Hsieh*: So you knew it could happen quite likely.

*Ferlinghetti*: Ya, right.

*Hsieh*: Are you still actively managing City Lights?

*Ferlinghetti*: No. My partner Nancy Peters was the head of the City Lights and managing editor for over 25 years. She retired last year and now Elaine Katzenberger is the chief operating officer and managing editor.

*Hsieh*: Have you ever had any plans to open a second or even a third City Lights bookstore?

*Ferlinghetti*: No. We had lots of offers, but a bookstore is not the kind of thing you can populate as a chain. We have such a unique personality that would be impossible to duplicate.

*Hsieh*: That's a good way to put it.

*Ferlinghetti*: I wouldn't want to duplicate it.

*Hsieh*: What's the main direction of City Lights now? Has it changed over the years?

*Ferlinghetti*: Well, it has broadened out more. You should talk to Elaine. She is away this week, but you can send her an email and ask her that question.

*Hsieh*: Next is a related question. How would you see City Lights fifty years from now?

*Ferlinghetti*: I have no idea of what it would be like.

*Hsieh*: You don't have any thoughts on that?

*Ferlinghetti*: I'm sure we will still be a dissident bookstore, dissident as opposed to the dominant culture. It's interesting to contemplate the idea that suppose the world could be changed in such a way that dissidents wouldn't have to be dissidents any more.

*Hsieh*: Yes, I see what you mean. Looking at your background, you went to France to get your Ph.D. How has that experience influenced you as a writer and as a publisher?

*Ferlinghetti*: I spoke French before English. I lived in France when I was a small boy. European publishers always published paperback books. So when I came back to the States 1950, I already had that in mind because that's what European publishers had always done. And a lot of the European publishers started as bookstores. Quite a few. Some of the biggest publishers in Germany, France and Italy started as bookstores.

*Hsieh*: By the way, City Lights is quite well known in Taiwan.

*Ferlinghetti*: Are you from Taiwan?

*Hsieh*: Yes, ages ago. How did you become an anti-war activist over the years?

*Ferlinghetti*: I was in the U.S. navy and I went to Nagasaki about six weeks after the bomb was dropped. And that made me an instant pacifist.

*Hsieh*: That must have been quite a shocking experience.

*Ferlinghetti*: Yes, it was.

*Hsieh*: It seems that you continue to challenge the definition of what art is. Is that a fair statement?

*Ferlinghetti*: Yes, but I'm not really a revolutionary artist because my art is quite traditional like I'm still drawing from the models. On the other hand, the content of what I'm painting is dissident.

*Hsieh*: So that's pretty much in line with the philosophy of your bookstore and the type of poetry you write?

*Ferlinghetti*: Right. By the way, I have a show of drawings from models in Italian Culture Institute in San Francisco from September 10 to October 10 this year. Then I'm going to have a big show in Rome next spring.

*Hsieh*: In the introduction to your book *Americas – Book I*, the editor described you as an elder maverick of American poetry. Do you think that's a fair description?

*Ferlinghetti*: I don't know about that.

*Hsieh*: In that book, there seems to be different stuff in terms of content. What did you try to communicate there?

*Ferlinghetti*: It's an epic poem. It goes up to the Kennedy assassination. And the second book, Book II, goes West.

*Hsieh*: I have not seen Book II yet.

*Ferlinghetti*: Well, I'm still working on it. I don't know when that would come out and who knows if it will ever come out. And the last book, Book III, would be on San Francisco. That's the last frontier.

*Hsieh*: That makes sense and I would be looking forward to that. How would you describe your relationship with the other Beat movement poets?

*Ferlinghetti*: I wasn't the Beats. I got associated with the Beats by publishing them. I was Allen Ginsberg's publisher for practically all of his life. I was his editor for all of his books up to his last book when he was bought out by Harper Collins in New York. So the Beats were our main successes as a publisher, but they were only one group, one generation of dissident writers that we published. We also published works of other dissident writers that weren't part of the Beats like Charles Bukowski and Sam Shepard, the playwright. Today our list edited by Elaine Katzenberger includes many radical books from south of the border.

*Hsieh*: But I think your relationship with them went beyond publishing. You provided City Lights as a meeting place to help nurture the movement. Right?

*Ferlinghetti*: That's true. They came and went. They were here quite often. Allen Ginsberg and Gregory Corso were here a lot. Kerouac wasn't here very often.

*Hsieh*: Looking back on the Beat movement, how would you characterize its effects on the society? Do you consider it an agent of change?

*Ferlinghetti*: Oh, definitely. It's as important as the Rock revolution was in music.

*Hsieh*: That's a good way to put it. I would like to ask you as a poet a couple of more questions. How can we attract more people to poetry?

*Ferlinghetti*: (Laughing) Write more comprehensible poetry. For instance, I just got a copy of a local little magazine by very young poets, about thirty or thirty five of them. The magazine has lots of self expression, but very little communication.

*Hsieh*: I know what you mean. I think it's easier to write poetry that is not comprehensible than to write something that is communicable.

*Ferlinghetti*: That's right.

*Hsieh*: Your poetry anthology *A Coney Island of the Mind* has been extremely popular. Could you talk about the background behind which you came up with those poems?

*Ferlinghetti*: Quite often people wanted to illustrate my poems with graphic pictures of the actual Coney Island. I keep telling them the book is not about the geographic Coney Island, it's about a state of mind. It's about an analogy of the world as Coney Island, but not the geographic Coney Island.

*Hsieh*: I see. With that, I want to thank you for your time.

# Maxine Kumin

(Credit: John Hession)

Born in Philadelphia, Pennsylvania in 1925, Maxine Kumin was a pioneer among the modern American woman poets. She had close interactions with fellow poet Anne Sexton in 1960s and 1970s.

Although she did not start writing poetry seriously until the age of thirty-two, her poetry won her many awards including American Academy and Institute of Arts and Letters Award and Pulitzer Prize in Poetry for her book *Up Country*. She published nearly twenty poetry collections (including *Connecting the Dots* and *Selected Poems (1960 – 1990))* and more than thirty books of novels, essays and children's books.

Her poems are deceptively simple, direct, focused and accessible and reflect her deep love for and intimate familiarity with the animals, vegetation and the land. She and her husband actively maintained a 200-acre farm in New Hampshire for almost four decades.

Kumin was appointed the Poet Laureate of the United States in 1981. She passed away in 2014.

The interview was conducted by emails with Ms. Kumin's reply dated February 13, 2010. Preceding her reply was the following remark: "I was quite bemused to receive two cc. of your poetry quarterly but was able to enjoy the photographs, especially the one of Roald, with the holograph of part of his poem. He audited a poetry workshop I taught at MIT many years ago and we became friends there. He visited my husband and me at our farm in New Hampshire that summer and I subsequently had dinner with him in Ithaca, New York when I was there as visiting poet just a few years ago."

*Philip Hsieh*: Could you sum up your philosophy on nature in your poems?

*Maxine Kumin*: I'm not sure that I have a coherent "philosophy" on nature. It is certainly true that many of my poems come up out of the earth we live on and from which we harvest all our own vegetables. We have been stewards of the land here (100 acres, most of it now in conservation) for more than forty years, keeping the pastures fertilized and limed, and mowing them at the proper intervals to maintain good grass for our horses. We raised ten foals and trained them to be good equine citizens. So I probably have a closer acquaintance with the land than many poets. I am an avid wild mushroom forager; I also collect the wild fiddlehead ferns that come up along a little stream bed almost as soon as the frost is out of the ground. I suppose I could make a sort of grandiose statement about respecting the land; we garden only organically and I am an ardent supporter of all green movements. Out of this respect also comes my desire to help protect the last herds of wild horses in the West, where the Bureau of Land Management is in the pocket of the big cattle ranchers who would like nothing better than to eliminate the last horses and take even that small holding to raise more beef cattle, which then go to filthy feedlots to be stuffed with grain before slaughter. . . you can see, I get carried away. My husband and I have rescued six dogs from shelters over the years and every one of them has been a care and a joy. They live long lives here. The two we are caring for today are each twelve years old and very active. Is that part of a philosophy of nature?

*Hsieh*: Could you elaborate on your views on aging and mortality as these two subjects surfaced quite often in your poems?

*Kumin*: Well, I am old now and obviously that is why aging and death surface so frequently in my poems. My view? Death is coming closer. We have had sixty-three years of marriage; selfishly, I hope to predecease my husband as I do not want to be the one who must go on alone. But we humans are simply part of the natural cycle; we are born, we live, we die. I am an atheist and I feel fortune not to be in the thrall of any religion. I was raised in the Jewish faith and I have a strong Jewish consciousness but I haven't been in a synagogue in fifty years. Also, consider: if we were immortal there would be no impulse to write poems. In a sense, all poetry is by its nature elegiac.

*Hsieh*: You've published at least 17 poetry anthologies over the span of nearly 40 years. That's impressive. How did you keep your muse coming and maintain such a high level of perseverance?

*Kumin*: Well, writing poetry is only a tiny ember now. I feel I have written what was important to me and I don't want to be an aged poet writing bad poems. My muse is on sabbatical, at least.

*Hsieh*: You did not begin to publish poetry until mid-life. Do you think beginning to write poetry later in life may actually give some advantages?

*Kumin*: Possibly starting in mid-life helps a poet avoid the glib romanticism of a tenderer age.

*Hsieh*: You've also published several novels, essays and children's books. Did you need to conscientiously switch your mode of creation when you approached different writing genres?

*Kumin*: No, I made no conscientious switch. The novels somehow came up out of leftover material that didn't belong in poems. The essays were for the most part commissioned by various publications. The children's books were, and still are, (see my brand new *What Color Is Caesar?*) a restoration of verve and pleasure. But all genres are words and I do not think that a poem is any different from a novel or a play because they all must develop in some way, following a narrative thread to closure.

*Hsieh*: You had a life-threatening accident in 1998. Had that event greatly changed your views on life and on writing?

*Kumin*: It was horrendous and I have a lot of residual neuropathy. But I don't think it had any impact on my views.

*Hsieh*: You once commented, "For me, my life is a metaphor for my work." Could you elaborate on that?

*Kumin*: That's an oracular statement, one I find difficult to parse. Essentially, I mean that everything I write comes out of the reality of my dailiness. I'm not capable of pithy philosophizing. I steer clear of mysticism. My hands and my heart are in the dirt.

# Jerry Ball

(Credit: H. Philip Hsieh)

Though Jerry Ball, born in Nebraska in 1932, received his degrees in mathematics, his insatiable curiosity for things around him and his immense desire for understanding different cultures are quite evident. He has a wide range of interests in literature and art: poetry, music, philosophy, religion and language.

Ball has had an intense interest in poetry since high school and is forever an enthusiast for haiku. He always carries a small notebook to capture those haiku moments. His memory capacity for poetry is incredible and has become a source of inspiration for people around him.

He writes poems both in the metered format and in free verse. His more than ten published books of poetry and haiku include *World between Mirrors*, *A Second Look* and *Baseball Seasons*.

The interview was conducted face to face at Rossmoor Café (Walnut Creek, CA) in two sittings: one on February 26, 2013 and the other on April 2, 2013.

*Philip Hsieh*: Jerry, my first question is this. You were so much immersed in poetry. How do you make poetry an integral part of your life?

*Jerry Ball*: By practice. Take time for poetry. There is a Buddhist writer and poet Jack Kornfield. When he talks about spirituality, it's more than just religious belief. "What is your spiritual practice?" he asks. Poetry to me is spiritual practice and other things as well.

*Hsieh*: How did you first become interested in poetry?

*Ball*: Probably the first interest I had in poetry was from an old 78 rpm record of H.M.S. Pinafore by W.S. Gilbert and Arthur Sullivan. I learned the words and recited to my friends. They thought it was funny. And so I liked that. So humorous thoughts and humorous poetry drew me on. Then I became interested in the poems of Robert W. Service. He wrote poems about Yukon, Canada. I was in the third to the sixth grades when I was doing that.
In college I went to San Jose State and studied Mathematics and Philosophy (emphasis in Philosophy of Language, notably Wittgenstein and Santayana). My interest in logic and language moved me toward poetry, and I studied with Prof. O.C. Williams with emphasis in 19th century British poets: Keats, Shelly, and Mathew Arnold; American poets: Eliot, Cummings, Frost, etc. My graduate work was with Prof. John Summers at Cal State Hayward, with a focus in symbolic logic, and structures of language, notably metaphor, and linguistic structures.

*Hsieh*: How did you get into haiku?

*Ball*: I taught poetry at Las Positas College in 1975. And one of my students named Bobby Laiser went to San Jose to hear a haiku group. She invited me to come. Kiyoshi Tokutomi was the haiku teacher. He got me stimulated and I have been writing haiku ever since 1977.

*Hsieh*: There is a book called *Haiku Mind*.

*Ball*: Yes, by Patricia Donegan.

*Hsieh*: Is there really such a thing as a haiku mind?

*Ball*: Well. I think so. It supports your spiritual practice. If you practice writing haiku, then you can develop your haiku mind. Haiku mind is the possibility, the same as the musical mind, or the ballet mind. Haiku is the practice, and so you have the mentality that goes along with it.

*Hsieh*: Is that a prerequisite of writing haiku?

*Ball*: You build a little at a time. And sometimes you are not sure what you are doing. But you produce it over and over again and it eventually develops.

*Hsieh*: You write both haiku in English and western poetry. Do you treat them differently in terms of the writing process?

*Ball*: Well. Because of the form itself, with haiku I have a small notebook in my shirt pocket which I carry with me all the time. I can produce haiku very quickly. With the longer English poetry such as sonnets or free verse it takes much more time, although I do edit my haiku. But I also spend a lot of time editing my longer verses. Sometimes you get a new insight in the poem and it will take a whole new direction. That's certainly true with haiku.

*Hsieh*: You've taught mathematics, philosophy and religious studies for years. How have those influenced your way of writing poetry?

*Ball*: Everything. They built my vocabulary. They showed me different perspectives. So I can write from the mathematical perspective or from the humanistic perspective. And in the long run they are all the same. Like Hindu says, all the religions are really one.

*Hsieh*: Have you actually written poems that are related to mathematics?

*Ball*: I have written poems that were related to mathematical reasoning.

*Hsieh*: So when you are teaching or writing about mathematics, do you have to consciously turn on your left brain a little more than your right brain?

*Ball*: Mathematics has an aesthetics sense, which a lot of people don't recognize. Mathematics to many people is just techniques. It isn't just techniques, It's soul, soul of the universe and the language of the universe. It's dear to me. It takes you to different places.

*Hsieh*: If someone asks the question about the practical uses of poetry. What would be your answer to the question?

*Ball*: Feeling better. You can get inside into yourself. You can sometimes remove yourself from doing foolish things. A good intention of poetry makes your mind open to the possibility of that being the case.

*Hsieh*: What is the heart or the essence of poetry?

*Ball*: Music. The Princeton Encyclopedia of Poetics divided western poetry into three types: the lyrical, the dramatic and the narrative. And all these are ways we have of interpreting our lives. So it's a way of seeing how we live.

*Hsieh*: Have you been exposed to Chinese poetry?

*Ball*: Well, I don't read Chinese, but I've read some English translations of Chinese poetry. And since I know haiku, I know something of Chinese poetry. The way I see it, poetry in Japan was a follower of Chinese poetry. Poetry was classically developed in China and then transferred to Japan.

*Hsieh*: How did you become interested in Buddhism?

*Ball*: I was sick and nearly died when I was 17. I had virus pneumonia and had a violent reaction to penicillin. After that, I found I liked the Buddhist character. I dislike being told by Christians how to think. The Buddhists, as a rule, don't tell you to think in a given way. The eight-fold path was a reasonable path to me.

*Hsieh*: You had a poetry collection entitled *Pieces of Eight – Haiku Offerings Along the Eight-Fold Path*. Was that primarily for young readers?

*Ball*: Not necessarily. Young readers only in the metaphorical sense of the word. It was for new readers.

*Hsieh*: Jerry, you've taught poetry for a number of years. What would be your recommendation on the best approach to reading poems?

*Ball*: Be flexible and be interested. And if you find a poem that you are interested, read it and read it thoroughly. Try it a number of different ways. Try to read it out aloud and try to read it in quiet by yourself. Different poems are adapted to different styles of reading. Find out what you can about the poet. Find out what you can whether there is a form, for example, a sonnet. And learn something of the history of the poet and some of the characteristics of the poet. So there could be a collection of classes just devoted to reading poetry.

*Hsieh*: And what about writing poems?

*Ball*: Write what you care about and write something you know about. Who are you writing to and who are you writing for? You might be writing poems on behalf of your parents or someone you admire or dislike.

*Hsieh*: You majored in mathematics and philosophy in college and graduate school. And yet your love for poetry and music is so intense and broad. How did you travel consciously between these two seemingly different worlds? That is, science on one hand and art on the other?

*Ball*: I just spent time and do it. It never occurred to me to do anything else. Teaching math and teaching poetry is recreation to me. I love what I do. When I teach poetry, I meet people who are interested in poetry and they produce poems. That's wonderful. I spend a lot of time at it.

*Hsieh*: Do you write poetry every day? Could you talk about your typical process of writing from conceiving the ideas to submitting manuscripts for publication?

*Ball*: At the peak of my writing long poems, I've probably written four or five hundred of them, I would write almost every day. What I do now is I write haiku almost every day. And I have many of this kind of pocket books in my pocket.

*Hsieh*: Do you write at certain times of the day?

*Ball*: I can write anytime.

*Hsieh*: You must have a comprehensive collection of poetry in the form of books and CDs. Could you describe the scope of your collection and your pride and joy?

*Ball*: There are certain poets I like. I like Robert Frost a lot. And I like Mary Oliver, Wilfred Owen, 19th Century British poets and Japanese poets such as Buson. I also like Chinese poetry although I do not know much background of Chinese poetry. I have recordings of about eight hundred poems, really classical poems. Among the recording poets, Dylan Thomas is a wonderful reader of poems.

*Hsieh*: I think one of the things that impressed me most about you was your enthusiasm and intensity in poetry and how you want to share that enthusiasm with others. That enthusiasm can be contagious. Where does that enthusiasm come from?

*Ball*: I don't know. It's just there. Sort of like eating chocolate. After a couple of bites, you begin to like it. Part of it is from other people. Part of it comes from the intrinsic value of the thing. I heard poems I like, and they got me stimulated.

*Hsieh*: Your memory is out of this world. How do you do that?

*Ball*: I don't know. I'm finding I'm losing it. Memory is part ability and part practice. You just practice to remember things. You can train your memory.

*Hsieh*: Do you recite poems from time to time? Even talk to yourself?

*Ball*: Yes, when I drive a car I will sing operas. [starting to sing some operas] I used to practice that when I drove to teach an evening class at San Jose State College. I put a CD in the car's CD player and then I would sing along with the record. So music and recording had a lot to do with my memory.

*Hsieh*: You have been very dedicated to teaching poetry and very active in organizing conferences and societies related to haiku. Could you talk about what motivated you to do all those?

*Ball*: Just seemed to me the right thing to do. I have certain abilities. One of the abilities is to organize conferences. I organized a lot of conferences and enjoyed being in the conferences. And I think good things happened because of that. It just feels right.

*Hsieh*: Thank you for your sharing and your time.

*Ball*: My pleasure.

# William Marr

(Credit: Stone Lee)

Dr. William W. Marr was born in Taiwan in 1936 and came to the United States in 1961. After receiving his Ph.D. in nuclear engineering, he worked in this industry.

Besides his career in engineering research, Dr. Marr has written modern poetry in Chinese and translated more than a thousand poems from English to Chinese. His translations cover such American poets as T.S. Eliot, Era Pound, William Carlos Williams, e.e. cummings, Robert Creeley, Lawrence Ferlinghetti and Ted Kooser. Regarded as one of the leading contemporary Chinese-language poets, he began writing poems in English in the early 1990s and has published four collections in English including *Autumn Window* and *Between Heaven and Earth*.

The late U.S. Poet Laureate Gwendolyn Brooks once commented about Marr's poetry "The accents and nuances are strange to me -- and refreshing." Marr served as the President of the Illinois State Poetry Society in 1993-1995. He has actively engaged in painting and sculpting and has had a number of solo and group art exhibits since his retirement in 1996.

The interview was conducted by emails with Dr. William Marr's concluding reply dated September 6, 2015.

*Philip Hsieh*: When and under what circumstances did you start participating in local poetry activities after you came to the United States? Did you have any memorable episodes?

*William Marr*: The first few years, I was so busy with my school work and the establishment of my engineering career and my family, that there was not much leisure time for me to focus on poetry. Then things started to settle down, and it happened that my friend Bai Chiu, who was a well-known young poet and the editor of Li Poetry Bimonthly in Taiwan, asked me to translate contemporary American poetry for his magazine on a regular basis. Along with my translations, he also published some of my poems. Later, he told me that poets and readers were asking, "Who was this Fei Ma?" (my Chinese pen name). They seemed quite excited, yet somewhat perplexed, by the sudden emergence of a rather mature, new poet.

My early poems were all written in Chinese. Later, I translated some of my Chinese poems into English, just for fun, and a few of them found their way into some poetry anthologies. These anthologies had rather fancy names, such as Yearbook of Modern Poetry, Outstanding Contemporary Poetry, Melody of the Muse--Best Contemporary Poetry, OCARINA'S Anthology of American and World Poetry 1978-79, LYRICAL VOICES, International Poetry Anthology, and Poetry International. However, I realized that the best language for writing poetry was one's own native tongue. As a result, I did not have much interaction with American poets. The only local poetry activity I participated in was a bilingual poetry reading sponsored by the Illinois Arts Council in 1981. Then one day in the early nineties, I read an article in the Argonne News, an internal publication of Argonne National Laboratory where I worked, about a physicist colleague who was also a poet. I was so excited that I called him on the phone right away and found that his office was in the building right next door. He was equally excited and asked me to show him some of my poems. The meeting was very warm and pleasant. He invited me to join the Illinois State Poetry Society, of which he was an officer, as well as a poetry workshop that he had organized. The Illinois State Poetry Society is part of the National Federation of State Poetry Societies. Our Society met once every other month, mostly to critique fellow members' poems, and occasionally to organize poetry readings in hospitals, senior centers, and schools. I was elected to serve as the Society's president from 1993 to 1995. I have been participating in poetry activities in the Chicago area ever since.

*Hsieh*: What motivated you to write and publish your books of poetry in English?

*Marr*: Soon after joining the Illinois State Poetry Society, I joined the Poets' Club of Chicago, and continued to translate my Chinese poems into English. But I was not overly ambitious about publishing my poems at that point because I knew it was not easy to publish poetry books in the U.S. It was a fellow at Argonne who encouraged me to publish my work after reading my poem, "Birdcage", which reminded him of his parents' situation in Lithuania. He was so enthusiastic that he was willing to share in my self-publishing costs. I was grateful but did not accept his generous offer. Then I learned that the aforementioned physicist colleague was operating a small press to publish not only his own works, but also works of his fellow poets. So, in

1995, I put together a book of poems, designing the book cover with one of my own paintings, and, with his help, found a printing house. This was *Autumn Window*, my very first book of poetry in English. Glenna Holloway, the founder and the first-term president of the Illinois State Poetry Society, and Li-Young Lee, a young star in American poetry, wrote the prefaces to my book. Ms. Holloway also helped to have an article published about me and my book in the Chicago Tribune. As a result, the first printing of *Autumn Window* was soon sold out and was reprinted in 1996. Then, my interest shifted to painting and sculpting. It was not until 2010 my second book of poetry in English, *Between Heaven and Earth*, was published by a POD (print-on-demand) publisher in Baltimore.

*Hsieh*: Are there any differences between writing poems in Chinese and English, particularly in the way of finding the best words in their best orders and of your thought process?

*Marr*: I remembered Professor Yang, my English teacher in Taiwan, used to jokingly emphasize the difference between the two languages. He said, relative to the Chinese grammar, English sometimes "eats with its behind". As a matter of fact, not only language usage, but also culture differences and social customs contribute to different ways of thinking and expression. That's why, when I write a bilingual poem, it's generally not a one-to-one translation, but a process of re-creation. Gwendolyn Brooks, former Poet Laureate of Illinois, once said something like "The accents and nuances are strange to me – and refreshing" about my poetry. I took it as a rare compliment.

*Hsieh* : How about the difference in their ways of selecting materials?

*Marr*: In general, people respond differently to certain events or circumstances due to their different cultural backgrounds or upbringings. Some newcomers to this country are baffled by some of the American jokes. Likewise, something that may be heart-stirring to people of one country might mean nothing at all to people of another country. However, I believe that one can always find something deep within an object or an event that can touch a person's heart regardless of his or her race, religion, culture, historical background, age, gender, or profession. The mission of a writer is to discover the inherent quality of things and the broad sense of humanity, and to find some effective way to express them. A work so created, I believe, can maintain its artistic appeal and be appreciated by any reader through the process of translation, regardless of the original language in which it was written. This has always been one of the important considerations that I have when writing a poem.

*Hsieh*: Most of your poems are very concise, and you like to use short lines in both of your Chinese and English poems. Why?

*Marr*: There are several reasons. First, working full-time did not permit me the luxury of time to write long poems. But more importantly, short poems are my perception of what poetry should be. Each poem is a universe in itself. Many good examples can be found in classical Chinese poetry.
But the main reason that I write short poems can be traced to my translation of works by the imagist poets such as Stephen Crane, William Carlos Williams, Richard Aldington, Adelaide Crapsey, and e. e. cummings.

Generally, my line breaks are based on the following considerations: (1) to enhance the inner rhythms; (2) to highlight or emphasize certain words or phrases; and (3) to create poetic ambiguities or multiple meanings.

For example, in my poem:

*BIRD CAGE*

open
the
cage
let the bird fly

away

give
freedom back
to the
bird
cage

the use of spaces before and after the word "away" is an attempt to create the feeling of openness and freedom. Additionally, the separation of "bird" and "cage" at the end of the poem is intended to create some unexpected or multiple meanings, thus evoke a feeling of shock or surprise. People are so used to thinking about the freedom of the bird, not the cage.

*Hsieh*: Let me change the subject. As an engineer, do you think your technical training and background have helped or hindered your poetry writing?

*Marr*: I don't think my career as an engineer has had much negative effect on my poetry writing. If anything, my technical training and background have given me the knowledge and wisdom to better observe and understand life in the universe. In fact, many critics have pointed out that the refined qualities that they often find in my poetry can probably be attributed to the scientific training that I received. If nothing else, my engineering career provided a stable and worry-free environment for my writing. People often wonder how I was able to engage in my scientific research and literary creation at the same time. They must have thought that these two realms were not compatible and were in conflict with one another. To the contrary, I found that they could complement each other. The scientific training simplified and purified my poetry, making it more objective and less sentimental. On the other hand, through poetry, I was able to consider problems at work from various angles, without confining myself or getting into a blind alley. Whenever I encountered difficulty or felt tired or frustrated in one realm, I would go to the other realm to take a break, to restore my energy, and to start anew. More importantly, because I knew there was always a backup available, I wouldn't feel too much pressure and, as a result, wouldn't worry too much about personal gains or losses. This kind of attitude, I believe, is especially important for a writer.

*Hsieh*: Have you ever tried using themes of science in your poetry?

*Marr*: Several years ago, a Chinese-American scientist living in the East Coast hosted a "Science Poetry Column" in Beijing's Poetry Magazine and asked me to send him some poems on this topic. "Two Suns or More", "Super Lightspeed", and

"Gravity" were some of the poems that I submitted. However, these poems are more poetic than scientific.

*Hsieh*: Your poetry is very simple yet profound and your choice of words is refreshing. How do you manage to do it?

*Marr*: This has a lot to do with my idea of poetics. I always feel that the best challenge to a modern poet is to use the simplest form with the fewest words to express the deepest, strongest feeling. I don't believe that the language of modern poetry needs to be difficult, obscure, or fragmented. A creative poet can always extract something from everyday life and purify it into the language of the times that can be understood, appreciated, felt, and enjoyed by everybody. I try my best to let each of my poems have its own form, its own voice, and its own life. Through poetry, it's possible to discover new meaning and new beauty in everyday objects. If my poetry can help someone recall or rediscover a happy moment in his or her life, bring back a beautiful scene or memory, show him or her that the world is still full of interesting and exciting things and that it is so beautiful and so wonderful to be alive, then I think I have succeeded as a poet.

*Hsieh*: Let me ask you this: How do you keep the balance between subtleties and obscurity?

*Marr*: I try to put some humor in my poems whenever I can, although I find it's not an easy task to keep the right balance. One slip and an intended humor could turn the poem into doggerel. By the same token, I find the relationships between subtleness and obscurity, intellectuality and sensuality, are all very tricky. How to find a balance point will largely depend on the perception and artistic cultivation of the poet. There does not seem to be an easy way except to read more, write more, think more, and experiment more.

*Hsieh*: Many of your poems carry the spirit of social concern and criticism. How do you keep the balance between story-telling and preaching?

*Marr*: People like to listen to stories instead of being preached at. This is because stories are usually fun and lively, while preaching can be dull and boring. A story can enter the mind, while a lecture or preaching often can only wander outside its door. A poem that can't move the poet himself can never move its readers or win their hearts. Therefore, I always try to tell stories instead of lecturing in my poems. Again, the balance between them is quite delicate.

*Hsieh*: Take your poem "Neckties" as an example. It starts from everyday life, then by introducing virtuality into reality, it leads the readers into the realm of spirituality. How do you keep the balance between virtuality and reality so as to arouse an aesthetic feeling?

*Marr*: Sometimes fiction or virtuality is more real than reality itself. This is because reality usually only shows the superficial aspect, while fiction or virtuality can enter into the core and explore the true meaning of things. Let virtuality and reality mix and interact within a poem so that it is closely linked to the real world and the intangible, where readers can find the door to appreciation and won't feel dull or left out. Alternatively, such a poem can usually trigger the process of association and imagination, and thus enable readers to share the joy of creation. A Chinese critic once pointed out that there are two unique characteristics of my poetry. One is the "long-distance design" which hides virtuality in reality. This allows a poem to escape the confinement of reality and broaden its domain. The other is the "incompleteness or inconclusiveness" which can lead a reader to embark on his or her own exploration. The reader can thus enjoy the pleasure of making his or her interpretation and complete (or create) the poem in his or her own unique way.

*Hsieh*: Talking about aesthetics, can you summarize briefly your aesthetic principles?

*Marr*: To me, a good poem is one that performs. A poet's job is merely to provide a stage, or a scene, and letting the characters or events in the poem inspire the readers' imagination to take flight and develop their own dramatic play. The scene could be a life episode, a personality snapshot, a dialogue, or a sketch of mind landscape. There is no need for any reasoning, self-righteous interpretations or conclusions from the author. Depending on one's personal experience and the mood at the moment, a reader can acquire his or her own perception from the scene. Such a poem is a living poem, a growing poem, a timeless and tireless poem. A reader once told me that every time he read my poems, he seemed to discover some unexpected new meanings. I told him that this was my intention.

*Hsieh*: Well said. Another related question: How do you find an appropriate metaphor for your poem?

*Marr*: Standing at various locations and viewing from different angles, I observe, ponder, and revise until it is complete in my mind.

*Hsieh*: Take your poem "Birdcage" again as an example. You seem to think things out in an unconventional way, sometimes even in a direction opposite to the normal thought process, and provide a surprise ending. Did you have the conclusion in mind when you started writing the poem? Or did it come as a sudden enlightenment?

*Marr*: More often than not, it comes as a sudden enlightenment. The first draft is usually not very rich in poetic quality. Through the revision process, it becomes more and more concentrated and focused. Finally, it all falls into place. Recently, I have started writing bilingual poems. The translation process (either from Chinese to English, or vice versa) has become part of the revision process. It is quite interesting to be able to more clearly see defects or imperfections in a poem written in one language from the standpoint of another language, and to find some way to enrich the languages and eventually improve the poem. Of course, there were poems that started with rather mature images. They usually came naturally in the wee hours of the morning, arising out of a long fermentation process in my mind.

*Hsieh*: That's interesting. My next question is this. Concern for humanity seems to guide most of your writing. Is it conscious or subconscious?

*Marr*: I have written very few ideological poems. I strongly agree with the American critic who said, in effect: "When a poet writes of a certain topic in his mind, it is quite possible that poetry has become the tool of opinion, not a way of exploration." Whenever something touches my heart, it motivates me to write. The concern for humanity is part of my nature. It arises in my poetry from the subconscious.

*Hsieh*: I'd like to touch on the aspects of your writing poetry. Which poets have influenced you in your poetry writing?

*Marr*: I have translated over one thousand foreign poems into Chinese, most of them are works of American, British, and European poets. Some are Latin American poets. Among them, T.S. Eliot, Baudelaire, and Ezra Pound seem to stand out. I especially love Eliot's poems. To me, his poetry has the most poetic flavor. Some of his thoughts on tradition and poetry have also won my heart. Between 1965-66, I translated and published several of his poems in *Modern Literature* in Taiwan. All of these poets have made their own unique and important contributions to the development of modern poetry. I have many favorite American poets. They include Emily Dickinson, Robert Frost, Carl Sandburg, William Carlos Williams, and e.e. cummings; the Imagist poets Richard Aldington, Adelaide Crapsey, Stephen Crane, and Robert Creeley; and the Beat poets Lawrence Ferlinghetti and Gregory Corso. Among them, William Carlos Williams has influenced me the most. Carl Sandburg's social concern and his love for ordinary people have also contributed greatly to my literary development.
Among the foreign poets whose works I translated and published in *Li Poetry Magazine* in Taiwan, C.P. Kavafy (Greece), Nazim Hekmet (Turkey) and the surrealistic poet Jacques Prévert (France) are the ones who have influenced me the most. As for the ancient Chinese poets, Du Fu, Li Po, Tao Yuanming, Li Shangyin, Li He, and Yang Wanli are among my favorites. Many years ago, a poet friend in Guangzhou, China, gave me a booklet, *Quatrains of Sceneries*, which he compiled and interpreted. The booklet consists of many beautiful classical Chinese

poems. I carry it in my car and read a couple of poems from it whenever I am out and have a few minutes to spare and enjoy.

*Hsieh*: Having written poetry for over fifty years, how do you keep your sensitivity sharp and fresh? What enables you to go on?

*Marr*: To me, poetry is life, and life is poetry. As long as there is a fresh stream in my mind, as long as I can hold an interest in life and curiosity towards the mysterious universe, and as long as I still possess a fresh and sharp feeler, then it probably won't be too difficult for me to keep the poetic juices flowing.

*Hsieh*: Since your retirement from your engineering profession, you have also engaged in painting and sculpting. Can you say something about the similarities and differences between these two art forms and poetry?

*Marr*: The biggest difference between poetry and painting, I think, is their realistic aspect. The medium used by poetry is our everyday language, which is accepted through common practice. Therefore, I feel that poetry (or literature in general) can't be too far from reality. If I use the word "eating" in my poem, even if it has a deeper meaning than the simple act of taking in food, it still should have something to do with eating. Otherwise, the readers will have no clue as to what you are talking about. Painting is different. It uses lines and colors as its medium. When I put a patch of red color on my canvas, it might represent a flower, the sunset, an excited face of a child, or the burning passion of a lover. So I feel that painting can be more surreal, more abstract, than poetry without creating too much of a communication problem. For those who know how to appreciate modern painting, they probably won't ask such questions as what an object in a painting represents, or depicts. We won't ask what is the meaning of a flower, a tree, or scenery. As long as they give us some sense of beauty, it is quite sufficient. I've found that sculpting sometimes possesses an even higher degree of casualness and spontaneity. It can thus satisfy even more of my desire to create. When written language hesitates or falls silent in front of some feeling or emotion, painting and sculpting often open up an alternate channel of expression for me.

*Hsieh*: Thank you for your elaboration. I would like to ask a final question. You have gained some conspicuous achievements both in art and in poetry. It seems that only a highly effective person can do that. How do you manage your time?

*Marr*: From 9 to 5, I concentrate on my research work. On evenings and weekends, I spend as much time as possible on my reading and writing. Many years ago, my family and I visited Yellowstone National Park. The earth-shaking waterfalls impressed me greatly. The following was one of the poems I wrote after the visit. It probably can be used as a footnote to my modest achievements accumulated over the years:

## THE LOWER FALLS OF THE YELLOWSTONE

without a doubt
the roaring sound
that shakes the sky and the earth
is heard by the creeks in the woods
and the snows at the mountaintop

but it does not seem to disturb
their steady paces

you can see
all the murmuring streams
are converging leisurely
towards the destined location
you can hear
the sound of melting
and transformation of the snows
so deliberate
speck by speck
drip by drip

# Roald Hoffmann

(Credit: H. Philip Hsieh)

Dr. Roald Hoffmann, one of the two winners of the 1981 Nobel Prize in Chemistry, was born in 1937 in Zloczow in today's Poland. He has been very interested in literature since college days, especially poetry. Since 1965 Prof. Hoffmann has been at Cornell University and he is now the Frank H.T. Rhodes Professor of Humane Letters Emeritus.

In addition to numerous honors in his profession, he is also an accomplished poet and playwright. He has published six poetry collections including *The Metamict State, Memory Effects* and *Soliton*. He has also written three plays. As a writer, Hoffmann reaches out to the general public with an interdisciplinary approach incorporating science, poetry and philosophy. He is fluent in six languages.

Hoffmann brings a fresh voice to the American poetic landscape with his deep understanding of science, his survival of Nazi occupation and love of art and words.

The interview was conducted at Cornell University campus on August 18, 2008.

*Philip Hsieh*: Roald, first of all, thank you so much for your generous time. I know you have many things to accomplish every day. I very much like to introduce technical leaders like yourself who also have significant accomplishments in the humanities. You held a professorship in Humane Letters at Cornell. What does it mean?

*Roald Hoffmann*: It means little, but I like the title because it means I'm not just a chemist. It reflects my interest. I have just retired; I think it's going to be given next to someone else who is unlikely to be a scientist.

*Hsieh*: Have you been involved in teaching humanities courses?

*Hoffmann*: No. Nobody asked me. But I have been asked from time to time by some faculty members in the English Department who knew me, to teach a week in their courses. I would do it if asked to teach humanities courses, but the Chemistry Department would not give me time off in the past. So I didn't do it. I taught introductory chemistry courses and loved it. For a few students, they will remember my interests outside of science, but for most of them, they just view it as a curiosity. That's the way the world is. It's OK. So this is also a definition of an optimist: When you see a classroom of 100 people. Thirty of them fall into sleep. Only two have their eyes lit up. Those two make the life worthwhile.

*Hsieh*: Do you see yourself as a bridge builder between the science and non-science worlds? What's the biggest satisfaction you get out of that kind of role?

*Hoffmann*: I don't have any such a grandeur feeling. I'm a very good scientist, an excellent teacher and a minor poet. I'd like to get to a certain stage of poetry. I'm not there yet. Yes, I'm a bridge builder. I like the metaphor of bridge builders. It gives me the feeling that I have the courage to try to build the bridge. It exposes myself in some way. There are positive aspects. I believe there are many scientists who have creative artistic activities in their lives. They, however, either supress or don't talk about them. The reason is they think maybe that will make other scientists think less of them. They hide it. Part of what I do is I bring people out of the closet. People may have a passion such as painting, jazz, etc. When they see I do those things, they tell me what they do. I look carefully at their offices which are revealing. Fortunately in America, things are pretty open. You don't have to hide your passion too much.

*Hsieh*: How do you divide your time between the two seemingly vastly different worlds? Are you a highly effective person when it comes to time management?

*Hoffmann*: I jump from here to there, and work too hard. No problem to moving between the worlds – I try not to separate them…Yes, I'm effective in managing my time.

*Hsieh*: Beginning in 1988 you were in residence at the Djerassi Foundation for three years. How did you immerse yourself in the literature world or in writing poetry in addition to your responsibility as a researcher and a teacher in the field of science?

*Hoffmann*: When I took a month off for the artist colony of Djerassi Foundation twenty years ago, I spent perhaps one hour a day on science. This past March-April, I went there again to rewrite the text of the play "Oxygen" for an opera version. I had a lot of time left. So I wrote 14 poems in that period of one month.

*Hsieh*: You said, "I write poetry to penetrate the world around me, and to comprehend my reactions to it." What are the underlying fundamental issues in life that you've been trying to uncover? And what kinds of satisfaction do you get out of writing poetry?

*Hoffmann*: How to deal with the end of love, how to deal with the loss in general, how to understand things that pull you in different directions and cause tensions. Sometimes just describing somethings or some feelings that are interesting.

*Hsieh*: Do you always like to play with words?

*Hoffmann*: I always play with words in English. Although it is not my native language, it's the only language I write. And I'm very good with words. God knows me better through poetry. I'm always a good writer. My science articles have been valued because they are clear and concise. Those are some of the qualities of value to poetry. Within the limits of the usual language that science has, I have a style in the science: the way science is done and the language. So I think there's a real connection between my poetry and my science. I'll give you an example. Recently I wrote an article about how the structures of discrete molecules evolve to a structure of solids. The question scientifically was: to what extent is the structure of the solids determined by the preferences in the structures of individual molecules. All of a sudden I got a good idea of calling this article "Solid Memory." We actually got it into print. That article has been noticed much more because of a two-word poem. What it summarizes is this: How does the solid remember the monomers? The conciseness is a value in science. That's an equation of words. The readers understand it. I don't have to explain it.

*Hsieh*: What do you intend to convey about the world of reasoning (science) and the technology world in your literary publications?

*Hoffmann*: I would like to humanize science, to show people that scientists are not different from other people. They are curious, but they are also full of passion, and concerned about the ethics of what they do.

*Hsieh*: Could you talk about your interest in literature at different stages of your life?

*Hoffmann*: Everything began in college, with great teachers in the humanities, poorer ones in the sciences. I kept reading poetry but did not begin to write poetry until I was about 40, and essays later.

*Hsieh*: Has it ever occurred to you that you might want to take up writing or humanities as a career?

*Hoffmann*: Oh, sure – many times I've thought I should stop the science and just write. But then science continued to be fun, and it still is. And it's easier to make a living as a scientist ! (smiling)

*Hsieh*: You are conversant in at least six languages. Could you talk about why languages are important in careers and in life?

*Hoffmann*: Languages are important. But I'm just a European, who was caught in a war as a child, a refugee. There was no option but to learn a new language. Or several languages. After a couple, others come easily. Struggling with a foreign language makes you sensitive to what an immigrant feels.

*Hsieh*: Your poems "The Golden Boxes of Forgetting", "June 1943" and "Games in the Attic" are all very touching to me. Do you mind talking about your childhood?

*Hoffmann*: Well, it's a question I thought about and asked myself a number of times. I grew up in that terrible time as a child. After we came to the United States, everything went right. I was a good student and was rewarded. I have talked to psychologists a few times in my life, but I never saw a psychiatrist. The psychologists have the natural tendency to trace things back to the childhood. I can trace some things in my behavior and my quality as a human being to that terrible time as a child. I'm still deathly afraid of authority in some way. Someone in uniform scares me and even waiters scare me. I laughed about it. I don't like to stand in front of a window at night. I've written a poem about this. I write my emotion in my poems. Sometimes your question is asked in another way: How can you be such an optimist given that you had so much suffering as a child? Well, I think the only reality is that some of us survived and others like my father did not. To me that survival is enough of a reason to be optimistic. I don't hate the Germans. I think somehow the act of survival gives us some meaning. The survivors would argue in two separate directions. They could turn into or away from religion. Some people would say that you survived and so you should thank God for it. Some others among the Jews who survived could never believe in religion again because they argued how god could stand silent while such evil was perpetrated. I don't think god was there when that happened. While the act of survival is a chance event, it is something to be thankful for. We survived due to the action of some good people. It is something to be celebrated in a way. I feel very positive about life although I am not happy about the loss of love (my father's death in the war) and the failure of my marriage to some extent. I'm generally positive, maybe something in my personality. Maybe we have to give credit to my mother.

*Hsieh*: How did you remember the details of your childhood to be put in your poems?

*Hoffmann*: I go back to remember them in the poems. Sometimes I feel bad because my memory is not good and that's not a good quality for a writer. One of the psychologists I talked to said, "Don't worry so much about the memory. As you write, some facts will come back to you. They are there in the subconscious." As I read the poems that contain the details to my mother, she said that's exactly what happened. It's a piece of advice here. It's OK to imagine the details. It took me sometime to write those poems about my childhood because it was painful. I'm in better balance now. I can not forget it. I could now cry for my father which I could not do before.

*Hsieh*: I like your poem "The Golden Boxes of Forgetting." Could you talk about it?

*Hoffmann*: It started out something imaginative and ended up with my father who was killed when I was five. There are three parts of the poem. The first shows strikingly how people can overcome their memories in rituals. All of a sudden, the second part is about volcanic landscapes of Hawaii. And in the third part my feeling came back.

*Hsieh*: What did you try to convey in the poem?

*Hoffmann*: I was thinking the problem in dealing with the past was that we needed to learn how to forget. We all have the intentions of forgiving, but it's not always easy. The poem was a good idea because something was original. It talked about forgetting. It could have emotional impact. On a personal level, it does not work that way. You create a ritual of forgiving, but the pain is much deeper. And you can not forget.

*Hsieh*: It's that conflict that makes the poem interesting.

*Hoffmann*: Yes. I got the idea of making the transition in the second part while walking across the volcanic areas in Hawaii and noticing how quickly the violence turned into green grass.

*Hsieh*: The second stanza told me there was hope in forgetting, but the final stanza gave it a twist that created tension and threw me off to some extent.

*Hoffmann*: Yes, it's just a boy who lost his father.

*Hsieh*: And how has your childhood inflenced your views on life and your career?

*Hoffmann*: The typical immigrant experience has influenced me. You don't know the language and the culture. You watch, you listen and you observe. Many immigrant children gravitate first to science and math where language is less important. It's easier to penetrate than laws, the arts and the social structures that require the controlled mode of expression.

*Hsieh*: What is your driving force for very actively writing and publishing poems and participating in poetry competitions? Did these mental activities provide new challenges outside the Nobel aura?

*Hoffmann*: It still gives me the same satisfaction as in my college days: It's the wonder of words and their meanings coming together. Simple words and complex meanings can have emotional impact. There is poetry and there is therapy. Poetry can be therapeutic. But real poetry is not psychological therapy. Real poetry is something you share with people you don't know. You also write for someone else. You want someone to read it. When I write, I'm trying to communicate. There is emotional value in poems, not new knowledge as in science. I try to understand philosophy at some level. I write poetry to this day and I also write plays and nonfictions. There is a kind of land between science, poetry and philosophy that I've made for myself. And I'm somewhere in the middle. Ideally I try not to separate them, but in reality I have to. I could not have published poems in scientific journals. But if I could,

I would. It's a very intellectual world I'm in here. It's not a world of Olympics. I love this world. It's a world made by the mind and a world that I could share across cultures.

*Hsieh*: How did you get into writing poetry as a life-long interest?

*Hoffmann*: It began at Columbia College, with a wonderful poetry reading course by the poet Mark Van Doren, and continued with meeting a great natural philosopher and poet at Cornell, A. R. Ammons. At Columbia, I was forced to take as in a typical American system a number of courses outside of science. Among those courses were art history, comparative literature and poetry reading. I loved them and also did well in the science courses. Somehow the world opened up to me in literature. I fell in love with poetry at the age of 19.

*Hsieh*: Could you explain how Van Doren got you excited about poetry?

*Hoffmann*: He did not teach us how to write poetry, that was not done in college in those days. He reviewed poems and revealed hidden depth in the words, the meanings not on the surface. And I thought that was just wonderful, very different from science. In science, if a word has several meanings, that is not necessarily good. Why was I not satisfied with the meanings in science? I was, but in poetry it adds the richness. It opened up a world of emotional meanings and somehow this was important to me.

*Hsieh*: What motivates you to write poetry?

*Hoffmann*: Trying to understand the world within me and around me. And the incredible richness of the English language.

*Hsieh*: What aspects of poetry attract you most? And why?

*Hoffmann*: I like the compactness of expression, the way words sound, how two words mean more than what they mean literally. I love the many (not one) meanings words evoke. One thing I like in English poetry is the power of short words. Long words are weak in general.

*Hsieh*: Could you talk about your experience in the poetry group at Cornell?

*Hoffmann*: Two in the group were professionals. We used to sit around over the coffee and listen to the master, A. R. Ammons who was teaching at Cornell then. It only took him a few minutes to write a poem while taking the rest of us a long time. We met once a week for a few years. Everyone got a poem and criticizing was mild and encouraging. It's something important for me because that's the first time I was able to get a consistent way to approach criticism.

*Hsieh*: And what about your interactions with another famous poet, Maxine Kumin?

*Hoffmann*: I took a course from Maxine Kumin on poetry writing at MIT in 1984. It's more like a workshop. It's the only course I took on poetry writing. She has been very nice to me. Her poetry is very different, almost all about nature.

*Hsieh*: Do you prefer certain poetic forms?

*Hoffmann*: I write in free verse. Within the constraints of modern poetry without rhyming, I try to put some sort of meter in the poems.

*Hsieh*: Do ideas and words come to you easily when you write poems or essays or plays?

*Hoffmann*: Most of the time, ideas come with difficulty. Once in a while I get a gift, a poem where words fall into place.

*Hsieh*: Do you complete a poem in one sitting or in different stages? And how do you know when a poem is done?

*Hoffmann*: It feels done. It usually goes through 10-20 drafts, except when there is this rare gift. In good working situations it can be done in one day. I tend not to revise too much. In the normal flow for me, I do 4 to 5 drafts by hand, then I have to type the manuscript and print it out. I just can't read on the screen. I then go through several more drafts on the paper. At some point, it falls into place. It's not yet finished. I know there are still a few drafts more to come. I usually go back a week later and make some more changes which are often small. It feels done. In this way, I must have written 300 or 400 poems, not all of them published though.

*Hsieh*: Do you allocate a set of time regularly to write poems?

*Hoffmann*: No, and that's a problem. I do the next thing that comes along. In that sense, I have not allowed sufficient time for the poetry. I do not do it on a weekly or monthly basis. I try every few years to go to a retreat for a month or so. It's best if I go away and if the place has some interesting nature. I often use the nature as a transition in the poems. I think the nature is full of metaphors. By immersing myself in nature, whether at a beach or a mountain, and looking in details of things, I begin to get into a frame of mind where I can look at other things and things within myself. I write things down while walking and looking at nature.

*Hsieh*: Nature generally represents familiar settings that the readers can relate and once you get their minds settle you can take them to more complex images.

*Hoffmann*: Yes.

*Hsieh*: Speaking of nature, in several of your poems, you had the images of wind and fire. Do wind and fire symbolize anything in your poems?

*Hoffmann*: Both symbolize change and that's more obvious with fire. I also like doors as a metaphor. They all symbolize passing from one place to another. Wind is also a symbol of power that's not visible but is strong. People usually don't see air as anything until they see a hurricane. Fire and its transformations are more obvious.

*Hsieh*: Does the image of fire relate to your childhood experience?

*Hoffmann*: Yes, indirectly.

*Hsieh*: In your mind, what kind of beauty in science moves you to write about it in poems?

*Hoffmann*: Science is a source of metaphors, of connections from one part of our life to another. It brings understanding. It's not exactly the beauty of science I want to bring to poetry. It is just the understanding of science.

*Hsieh*: What are some of the reasons to welcome more poetry that deals with science?

*Hoffmann*: There are metaphors in science that are somehow poetic. For example, catalysis is an interesting word that has many meanings. When I wrote my poem "An Unusual State of Matter," I just learned about a state of matter which even most scientists don't know. Someone just gave it a name "metamict". A very strong word. Once you find the definition of it, it's a poem by itself. It's a state of matter in which radioactive atoms with time ruin a beautiful structure. The enemy is within. I'll give you another example. The poem "Free Boundaries." Where did I get it from? I was listening to a theoretical chemistry seminar. The speaker was saying, "Let's solve the differential equations under the assumptions of free boundaries." I immediately wrote down "free boundaries." What a lot of potential meanings in those two words. He was talking about mathematical terms. Tension arises from two conflicting things: something being free and yet having boundaries. I said those words were very interesting. I was going to use them in poems.

*Hsieh*: Contemporary poetry is almost void of science. In the history of poetry, was this always the case?

*Hoffmann*: In English poetry, there was once a time (18<sup>th</sup> century) when a poet, Alexander Pope for instance, could and did write of the science of his time…

*Hsieh*: Do you write poetry to reach out to a wider audience than your scientific circle?

*Hoffmann*: A different audience, not necessarily a wider audience. The world of publication in poetry in America is rather small. Typically a book of poetry is published under one thousand copies. Funny thing is in other countries like Denmark or Israel with much smaller populations, they also publish 1,000 copies. These countries value poetry more. I do not include the lyrics of songs or pop music. Very few poets reach wider audience. Could it be that poetry is so complicated or too personal or too philosophical to be understood by the average readers?

*Hsieh*: Maybe poetry does not offer solutions and they are contemplative?

*Hoffmann*: Yes, you have to take the time to read poems.

*Hsieh*: How do you introduce the concepts and terminology of science to the general public who reads your poetry? And how to do it without the readers getting lost or without interrupting their flow of reading?

*Hoffmann*: Gently. It's one of the problems of working science in the poems. Usually when you read a poem, you don't have to understand every word. I'm sure that's true with other languages. Sometimes you can get a feeling or what I'd like to describe as "float on the words." You understand something, then you lose understanding and then all of a sudden you find the understanding again.

*Hsieh*: "Float on the words"?

*Hoffmann*: Yes, from a piece of understanding to another. I think if there are too many things you don't understand, you stop reading. You can't lose the readers entirely. But most of the time, if the subject is science, something turns on to tell you, this is science , you had better understand it, or you are stupid. Shall we blame that on some teacher? What a heavy burden to bear. I'd love it if people would give me the same privilege that they give to a person when talking about something very personal in the poem. You don't know what he's talking about and you go on a little bit. That's one of the difficulties of having science in a poem. People feel they have to understand it. They don't have to. They could sort of take it from the sounds or images.

*Hsieh*: When you write poems containing science, do you adopt a different frame of mind?

*Hoffmann*: No, though I may be "looking over my shoulder." Worrying that I get the science just right, just in case my colleagues should read my poems. I shouldn't worry.

*Hsieh*: Do you use science as a teaching vehicle for the non-science audience in some of your poems?

*Hoffmann*: No. I have been very interested in teachng the general audience about science. Nothing to do with poetry. I write many articles and write a column for American Scientists.

*Hsieh*: What do you see as advantages and disadvantages of a technical person to write poems?

*Hoffmann*: Well, the disadvantage is that science is prosaic, thinking of all exceptions. But all that metaphor in science is a definite poetic plus.

*Hsieh*: What recommendations do you have for scientists or technologists along the line of humanities and poetry?

*Hoffmann*: Well, the humanities and poetry give meaning to life. They do not solve, but they offer resolutions to the things/feelings of this world that science cannot touch. Poems provide spiritual satisfaction. Try to enter this world!

*Hsieh*: You've also written plays. Please comment on what motivated you to do that.

*Hoffmann*: Plays give me another way to express myself. I also love the interaction with actors and directors. Theater is really magical; a light goes off and on, some music, and you are 200 years away.

*Hsieh*: Please talk about your future plans on writings for the general and literary audience?

*Hoffmann*: I will keep on writing. It's about time to think about publishing another volume of poetry anthology.

*Hsieh*: Great. Thank you very much. I truly enjoyed our conversation.

# Ted Kooser

(Courtesy of Blue Flower Arts)

The Poet Laureate of the United States from 2004 to 2006, Ted Kooser was born in Ames, Iowa in 1939. Like Wallace Stevens, he spent much of his working years as an executive in the insurance industry.

Kooser has published twelve collections of poetry including *Sure Signs* and *Delights and Shadows* that was awarded the 2005 Pulitzer Prize in Poetry. He has also written books in essay including *The Poetry Home Repair Manual.* Among other awards he had received were the Pushcart Prize and the Stanley Kunitz Prize, as well as several honorary doctorates. His writing is known for its clarity, precision and accessibility. Much of his poetry focuses on the Great Plains.

He teaches in the English Department of the University of Nebraska and hosts a weekly newspaper program called "American Life in Poetry."

The interview was conducted by postal mails and Mr. Kooser's reply was dated February 8, 2009.

*Philip Hsieh*: You had worked in the insurance industry for thirty-five years. How has the business world affected your poetry and poetry writing?

*Ted Kooser*: Working every day with people who had very little interest in, or training in, poetry, helped me to write in a manner that is accessible to nonliterary people. I have a very good sense of how working people take literature into their lives, and had I spent my working years teaching at a university I wouldn't have developed this ability. My newspaper column, American Life in Poetry, which now has four million weekly readers, is also a product of my sense of the reading habits of ordinary working people.

*Hsieh*: When you were working, how did you find the time and the environment to write poetry?

*Kooser*: I got up early every morning, at 4:30 or 5:00, and wrote for a couple of hours before going to the office.

*Hsieh*: How have the vast landscapes and the life style in the midwest shaped up your poetry?

*Kooser*: I have never lived anywhere but on the prairies, and it was inevitable that those landscapes would be a setting for my poems, as they are a setting for my life.

*Hsieh*: Your poems have been known for their clarity, precision and accessibility. How do you maintain that clear, precise and accessible style while evoking your readers' imagination and sense of aesthetics?

*Kooser*: While I am revising my poems, extensively revising them, I almost always revise toward clarity and away from difficulty and obscurity. I want an audience that can understand what I'm writing, and I work toward assisting them.

*Hsieh*: You are known for plainspoken style and a gift for metaphors. From where and how did you derive your metaphors?

*Kooser*: I wish I knew from whence metaphors come, because if I knew, I could summon them up at will. As it is, though, they arise spontaneously and unexpectedly, and I seize upon them with great delight.

*Hsieh*: What do you think has developed from your *Valentine Poetry Project*?

*Kooser*: The valentine poems have always been mostly about pleasure, and I've enjoyed writing the poems and sending them out. And they've made me a lot of friends.

*Hsieh*: Could you talk about a couple of your poems that were most satisfying to you?

*Kooser*: Rather than to specifically address poems, I'd prefer to generalize. The poems I most like are the ones that, when finished, seem to have every element in the perfect position, every line ending, every punctuation mark. Every word is the best word, every rhythm the most appropriate rhythm. It is very difficult to write a poem at this state of perfection, but I am always striving to do so, and every revision is a step toward that end. I might revise a twenty-line poem forty or fifty times, then give up on it due to my inability to get it right.

*Hsieh*: What is the most important advice you could give to people who read and write poetry in the ever increasingly digital world, particularly young poets?

*Kooser*: My advice to young and beginning poets is to read. To read, read, read. One cannot write effective poetry without reading a lot of poems. I ask my graduate students at the University of Nebraska to read 100 poems for every one they try to write.

# Nikki Giovanni

(Courtesy of Nikki Giovanni)

Born in Knoxville, Tennessee in 1943, Nikki Giovanni took pride in her multiple roles as an African American, a daughter, a mother and an English professor. Her poetry is quite popular among the general public and expresses the dignity of African Americans, her experience in the Civil Rights Movement and her respect for family. Between 1960 and 1970, she and other African American artists founded the Black Arts Movement. She has been dubbed the "Princess of Black Poetry."

Giovanni is an avid supporter of slam, spoken-word and hip-hop. She has written close to twenty volumes of poetry including *Bicycles: Love Poems* and *The Collected Poetry of Nikki Giovanni* and several collections of essays and children's books.

As a recipient of over twenty honorary doctorates and numerous awards, Giovanni is currently a University Distinguished Professor teaching writing and literature at Virginia Tech.

The interview was conducted by postal mails with Ms. Giovanni's reply dated September 7, 2011. Preceding the reply was her note: "Thank you for your letter. My mother lived for over a decade in Danville so I know the area very well…and love it. I will answer your questions to the best of my ability and recollection."

*Philip Hsieh*: You have been a civil rights activist. How did you transcend the underlying anger and make it the source of inspiration for your poetry?

*Nikki Giovanni*: I don't think there is or can be any revoluntionary intent that is not filled with love. James Baldwin once said to be Black in America is to be filled with rage but I think he overstated a bit. There are frustrations and there is anger about injustice but not any sort of free flowing anger that allows you to dislike or disrespect the people. I'm neither filled with anger nor bitterness. I just refuse to look away from injustice.

*Hsieh*: In your mind, what would be a healthy way of looking at the issues of race and other forms of discrimination?

*Giovanni*: To me the only healthy way to look at anything is honesty. That will create and tap into other emotions, sadness, anger, frustration, etc., but you still, to keep yourself sane, have to honestly look and say "This Is Wrong" or perhaps even "We Should Be Better Than This."

*Hsieh*: As a founding member of the Black Arts Movement in the late 1960s, what was your own vision for the movement then?

*Giovanni*: My vision was a community in communication with itself and others. Again, the word I'm stuck with is Honest. If you honestly present your concerns there should be and must be compromise which should help us all go higher.

*Hsieh*: Your poem anthology *Bicycles* with a subtitle *Love poems* is about trust and balance. Could you elaborate on that?

*Giovanni*: But that's what a Bicycle is: trust and balance. You will fall at some point. Even as an adult; even as a professional rider …you will fall. In love that's true also. But you try to maintain balance and trust that if you balance it all it will work. I wrote a poem entitled "Balances" a longtime ago. I still believe that.

*Hsieh*: And how did you transform yourself from a young revolutionary to a poet so enthusiastic about love, many forms of love?

*Giovanni*: Revolutionaries are always about love. We love the people; we love a person; we love justice; we definitely love change. It's always love. If not love it's not revolution but rather some crazy cult that will have to be destroyed.

*Hsieh*: Despite many personal losses and life struggles, many of your books convey the idea that it's good to be alive. How do you keep your spirits up all the time? Does poetry provide you with the sort of strength to support that notion?

*Giovanni*: Golly, to quote Gomer Pyle. What better thing do we do than be alive? It's a great idea…Life. I highly recommend it.

*Hsieh*: Following the shooting massacre at Virginia Tech in 2007, you spoke to a large group of mourners at a coliseum. That must be an experience with complicated feelings. How did you come up with those comforting words and that chant poem at the end of the ceremony?

*Giovanni*: The airline pilots teach us so much. On the average day they take off and land. Then a storm comes or some other threatening thing, birds sucked into the jets and you have to land on a river, that sort of thing. The pilots say most days they "just drive the bus and park it. But today they had a bit more trouble." Poetry is like that. At a tragic moment I was asked to do something. I thankfully was able to drive the bus and park it. I could just as easily have crashed. I'm glad I didn't.

*Hsieh*: In an interview with Bill Moyers, you indicated that, as an artist, you're always looking for safe places. Where did you find them?

*Giovanni*: I don't and I probably never will. But I still look.

*Hsieh*: Could you name some of the writers who had inspired your writing, particularly poetry writing?

*Giovanni*: I adore the poetry of Gwendolyn Brooks and Langston Hughes. I guess I would consider myself a literary granddaughter of Hughes since we are all working off his decision to be a true voice of his community.

*Hsieh*: Does your poem "My Muse" say a lot about the confidence and clarity in your approach to poetry?

*Giovanni*: Yes.

*Hsieh*: Could you talk about the general process in which you conceive the ideas, complete the first drafts and go about the revisions?

*Giovanni*: Like all writers, painters, actors, well, artists, I'm always looking. You have to pay attention. Then when something strikes you have some of the tools at your command.

*Hsieh*: You are such an energetic and prolific poet. How do you make yourself so productive?

*Giovanni*: I'm always asking "Why Not"?

*Hsieh*: How do you view poetry slam?

*Giovanni*: I love The Slam. I just had the occasion to speak for ESPN at the annual HBCU Bowl Game in Orlando, Florida. My question to ESPN: Why is Poker, which is not a sport, on television and Slam Poetry, which is, not? When are we going to get our show on Break Dancing since we have shows featuring Synchronized Swimming? The Art Kids deserve a venue as much as the athletic kids do.

*Hsieh*: What would be your short invitation to poetry to reach out to the general public? And your advice to young poets?

*Giovanni*: Poets have to understand that we, like Opera and Ballet, are not going to be everyone's cup of tea. Don't let anyone make a false comparison of your art because they can make you feel like you have failed. And you haven't. My advice to young writers always is to write. There is a lot of unfairness out there but you have to do what you can. Don't worry about other people. Envy has no place in Art. Just strive for excellence.

# Juan Felipe Herrera

(Credit: University of California-Riverside)

Born to migrant farmworker parents in 1948 in Fowler, California, Mr. Juan Felipe Herrera is a poet, teacher, cartoonist, performer and activist. His poems often address social issues and his Chicano experience in the U.S. and challenge the borders between genres, styles and languages.

With more than a dozen collections of poetry to his credit, Mr. Herrera has received many awards including National Book Critics Circle Award in Poetry for *Half the World in Light*. Recent poetry collections included *Notes on the Assemblage*. He is an innovative and prolific writer and his creativity has left marks in many other fields: prose, short stories, children books, TV films, theatrical and musical performance and cartoons.

Mr. Herrera was elected a Chancellor of the Academy of American Poets and appointed to be Poet Laureate of California. In 2015 and 2016, he was named Poet Laureate of the United States. He currently holds the Tomas Rivera Endowed Chair in the Creative Writing Department as UC Riverside.

The interview was conducted through a few rounds of emails with the last email dated May 13, 2012.

*Philip Hsieh*: Your parents were migrant workers. How has your childhood experience helped shape your artistic pursuit?

*Juan Felipe Herrera*: My father, Felipe, a laborer, from a family of eight arrived in the United States before the Mexican Revolution of 1910. My mother, Lucha, a singer and farm worker, from a large family as well, in an exodus from Mexico City arrived in Juarez, Chihuahua in 1918 and after a year or so, moved to El Paso, Texas. In a sense, my parents represent the fusion of two worlds of incredible change and creativity. As a child growing up, every word they uttered and the stories they told became a template for my imagination, as we migrated through the agricultural fields of California and New Mexico – word art, social justice and simplicity. In honoring them through my writings and musicals for young people, it has been my hope to praise all those who work hard under sun yet go on without mention by the public at large. These days I write from these experiences and attempt to embrace everyone in my writing and if possible, to "task the void," as the great ancient Chinese master, Lu Chi, has said of literature's delights – a surprising and noble goal. How beautiful it all is – writing, life, human beings.

*Hsieh*: You had lived in Fresno, California for a long time and had said previously "Fresno has been for Latino/a children's writers what Paris was for Hemingway and Fitzgerald." Please explain this in more details.

*Herrera*: If only I could explain what brings artists together in one place and encourages them to create new things at the same time. Fresno is in the heart of California: an agribusiness capital and, in a way, a river-like ebb and flow of immigrant and migrant cultural communities – hard labor, few resources, border patrol, yet, a fountain of infinite possibilities for the cross-over of language, culture and community solidarity. Poets, children's book writers, many great Chicano, Latino and writers at large have risen from this area; all great friends: José Montoya, Gary Soto, Victor Martinez, Margarita Robles, Inez Hernandez Tovar, Andres Montoya, Philip Levine, Chris Buckley, Leonard Adame, Diana Garcia and many others. Today the new Fresno Hmong generation of writers is also making its voice loudly heard. Imagine that?

*Hsieh*: Many of your poems portray Chicano life and school moments in vivid details. What kind of messages do you intend to convey?

*Herrera*: Three things: I want to speak about my experience so that my writing will reach new young readers and speakers of Spanish and English and encourage them, through words, to face themselves, their family and history. As you know, these days, a number of Chicano and Latino literary works are being banned in Arizona. In the majority of schools in the United States our work is rarely mentioned unless there is a Migrant Education program in the area. There are exceptions, of course, and many teachers and administrators are doing their best, however, we face an uphill battle. When I write a children's book or a young adult novel, the interests of the publishing house and the editors can also become an obstacle. Nevertheless, a poem finds its way home on its own. Finally, I write with a joy for experiment, explosion and surprise. Too many messages make the work heavy and dull. Three messages are good: embrace others and yourself, honor your family and ancestors, and give of yourself to nature and all.

*Hsieh*: In the 1960s and 1970s you became immersed in the Chicano Movement. How has that involvement affected the contents and the forms of your poetry?

*Herrera*: The "Movement" was a highly unpredictable moment and a cradle for far-reaching dreams. This was good. In 1970, at the peak of the Chicano Civil Rights political and cultural rights and student movement, everyone talked about re-claiming our cultural history and practices. Instead of reading the rare books, I was inspired to lead a film, photography and documentary quest into the Lacandón jungles of Chiapas, to the coast of Veracruz and the mountains to Nayarit, Mexico. These were three major locations where indigenous communities live out their unique and similar life-conditions – Mayas, Totonacs and Huichol peoples. Some endangered, others in survival mode and in the case of the Huichol, we had a culturally robust group yet it had been and continues to this day to be pushed out into regions of refuge in mountainous areas with little food and water. Cultural story, I discovered, was not as significant as sovereignty and land. In terms of my poetry I made various attempts to speak of and for these communities, to also display photographic landscapes and to give lectures and workshops having to do with the "hidden" Mexico. Ultimately, the poem became a question of justice, culture and power and its shape was malleable given the audience and context.

*Hsieh*: You used the word "boundaries" quite frequently in your poems. Could you elaborate on its meanings and significances?

*Herrera*: Freedom, liberation, the tearing down of barricades, wire fences, passport lines, inspections units, green vans rolling into the fields in search of "illegals," questions by sheriffs and police and border patrols, being tested for proficiency in English – all this is very emotional for me. One of the first songs my mother sang to me during my childhood was "El Contrabando de El Paso / El Paso, Texas Contraband." This is a song about "illegal" Mexican workers that get apprehended by the border patrol at the El Paso borderline. At the age of six, across from our trailer, I witnessed the border patrol arrive at our little plot of land in Escondido and pull out my friends, the Garcías, one by one from the house they owned and stuff them into a deportation patrol van, never to be seen again. Freedoms are better than boundaries, don't you think?

*Hsieh*: How did you become interested in indigenous cultures?

*Herrera*: In a way, as a teen, I considered myself "indigenous." My mother also considered herself "india" or "Indian" as they say in English. This was a soft notion. There was something about my family; something that emerged from the Mexican earth and the lands of the USA too. No one in school or in the media ever mentioned it. But we knew it at home, on the outside of the day-to-day machinations of high society. Later, at the University of California in Los Angeles, as I said earlier, I wanted to more consciously re-connect and draw out and more fully grasp this mood, feeling and notion of being "indigenous." I did and it changed my life.

*Hsieh*: You have devoted a significant amount of time to teaching poetry in prisons. What's behind this?

*Herrera*: Poetry has something to do with the dynamic element of inner and outer life. Bringing poetry to prisons and "juvenile halls" and "continuation high schools" does wonders. People sing. They shout and smile. Some cry and remember things they have buried for decades. Others relive the past. Sometimes all that happens is a song where everyone listens as if they were standing in front of a long lost village of flowers. Poetry is my life. It is hard for me to live without it. And sometimes, I just get lost in thoughts or work.

*Hsieh*: Could you talk about how you developed the taste for poetry?

*Herrera*: My mother always sang to me. My father always told stories of coming to the United States when he was fourteen years old, how he jumped on a train from Chihuahua, Mexico and landed in Denver, Colorado. My parent's words were pure poetry. I don't know why; maybe because they spoke in parables or simply because all they owned were words. Powerful, lovely words.

*Hsieh*: Who had strong influences on your poetry writing? And how?

*Herrera*: Besides my parents being powerful influences, well, my uncles, Roberto and Vicente Quintana. Uncle Roberto was a radio-theatre pioneer in Juarez, Chihuahua in the 30's and a Spanish-English program founder in San Francisco in the '50's and '60's and a great comedian, poet and actor. Uncle Vicente was a rebel artist, a Surrealist painter in the 20's in El Paso, Texas and always devoted to his art. They were poor, so they invented everything they touched. My uncles were great sources of inspiration. Later, during high school, my great poet friend, Alberto Urista, who lived ten feet away from our tiny living room on 11th street in San Diego, California, became my poetry mentor. At first we shared the same bus to school, then later, when he became a national and international literary sensation, we shared poems, read our work together at events and lived in the "underground" bohemian poetry scene for a few years. While at UCLA in the late sixties, I was mesmerized by performance groups and concerts at the university. My influences are many – from New York's experimental theatre scene of the sixties to the last jazz musicians of the 50's still recording like Thelonius Monk. New waves of gurus from India, the popularity of Zen and Eastern thought – all these creative lenses of observing the self, the world and cosmos were key in my art and life.

*Hsieh*: Some critics considered you to be one of the first poets to successfully create a new hybrid art. What's your reasoning for this new approach?

*Herrera*: This is a difficult question. People and aesthetics, is the short answer. I believe in both. But there are many combinations – nature and people, aesthetics and text; the private and the public. The post-war Polish poets are a great example - Szymborska, what a great fusion of art and political voice. The Late T'ang poet, Li Shang-yin, is another magnificent example – love and aesthetic complexity. Philip Levine, our current US Poet Laureate – what clear crafted narratives and yet, there is something elusive and luminous in his work; this is what pleases me.

*Hsieh*: How is your typical process of writing poetry? Where do you get your sources of ideas? Do you complete first drafts in one sitting? And what about revisions?

*Herrera*: Thirty seconds. Immediate. Flow, do not stop and ponder. Do not erase; all is good. Let the pen lead you. Follow the ink. Disappear, then come back and open your eyes. Then play. One sitting. Two sittings are ok. The rest is polishing. Not too much or you will hurt the poem and make it wear ugly, heavy shoes. What you revise is the blank page, what you have not said. So you leave the page empty. It will come when ready. Sometimes I finish one hundred poems in three weeks. Sometimes it takes me three weeks to finish one. There is no rule.

*Hsieh*: Besides being a poet, you are a cartoonist and performer. How do you manage your multiple talents and their competition for time?

*Herrera*: They are all the same. That is the secret. Writing is my art. It leads me to performance. Breath is life, then movement. After that everything happens. I usually write everyday – on everything I can write on. Paper, cardboard, folders; envelopes are my favorites because they are long and thicker than paper. Starbuck's bags are magnificent when you are in an airport and do not have a journal. You untie the back, loosen it, tear it, and fold it into a seven-page booklet. Cartoons, music, art and writing were my friends in middle school.

*Hsieh*: Have you had any exposure to Chinese poetry?

*Herrera*: A little. My exposure to Chinese poetry, music and art probably comes from living in San Francisco and attending Stanford University in the late seventies. At the university, I met Francis Wong, musician, scholar and in many ways a key member of the Chinese and Asian music and arts "movement" in the Bay Area during the '80's to the present. I also have performed with Genny Lim, another pioneer in the poetry and performing arts in San Francisco. At the University of California in Riverside, I have met young poets from Beijing who handed me their work and told me about their writer friends and their love for poetry. In my undergraduate and graduate poetry workshops I have had Chinese poets who teach me quite a bit about China; its regions, mountains and life. Every day, it seems, I am more interested in China. Actually this was quite a topic back in the '60's. As Chicanos we wanted to have dialogue with the entire Americas, Asia and Africa. However, we lacked resources and networks. For quite a while, I have been extremely interested in the Taoist poets and thinkers. The Taiji Diagram drawn during the Ming dynasty by Zhang Huang, the Chinese scholar, is an incredible complex of thought, cultural knowledge and cosmology, as is the Star Chart of 1247, a stele, at the Confucian temple in Suzhou Jiangsu province. I saw the original text and stele at the Chicago Art Insititute's exhibit on "Taosim and the Arts of China." My favorite work was that of a Ming dynasty ink-on-silk drawing of "Zhuangzi Dreaming of a Butterfly" created by Lu Zhi. Who was the dreamer? Zhuangzi or the butterfly? The butterfly! Currently, I am very concerned about the ongoing plight of Tibet and its peoples, its sovereignty, its cultural life. You see how all this comes back to the same thing. Freedom. Poetry. Freedom.

# Christopher Herold

(Credit: Carol O'Dell)

Haiku, originating from Japan, has become a widely popular form of poetry in various languages in recent years, perhaps in part due to its emphasis on compactness and insightfulness. Christopher Herold, together with Alex Benedict founded in 1998 *The Heron's Nest* and had served as its first editor-in-chief for eight years. The magazine has become one of the leading English haiku magazines.

Christopher Herold was born in Suffern, New York in 1948. He is an accomplished musician and a practicing Buddhist, has published six volumes of haiku selections including *A Path in the Garden* and *Inside Out*.

The interview was conducted by emails with Mr. Christopher Herold's concluding reply dated May 26, 2012.

*Philip Hsieh*: How large is the haiku community in the U.S.? In your estimate, how many English-language haiku readers and writers are there in the U.S. today?

*Christopher Herold* : I can only take a guess at this. I do know that there were nearly 700 members of the Haiku Society of America in 2011. With the advent of internet and online journals, membership began to increase significantly back in the late 90s. But this figure doesn't really reflect how many people are reading or writing haiku here in the States. What it does represent is an approximation of those who are serious enough about haiku to have joined the largest, longest standing haiku organization in the West. I am certain that there are several hundred more such readers and writers who are not current members of the H.S.A. There are a number of independent groups who prefer not to get involved beyond their local meetings, and there are societies, like The Yuki Teikei Haiku Society of the U.S. and Canada who operate in their own environment. And, of course, there are poets who belong to more than one national group. So, my wild guess at the number of serious haiku practitioners in the U.S. would be around 1,200, give or take.

*Hsieh*: In your opinion, what has heightened the recent popularity of haiku in the U.S.?

*Herold*: It seems clear to me that the internet has been the single biggest reason haiku has proliferated as quickly as it has. Before the turn of the century, when the world-wide-web was still but a babe, there were only two or three on-line journals. Now there are many. Before the year 2000, most American haiku poets subscribed and submitted to the major hardcopy journals: *Modern Haiku* and *Frogpond*, as well as a few others such as *The Heron's Nest, South by Southeast, Acorn, Haiku Headlines, Geppo, Woodnotes,* and *Hummingbird.* There were earlier journals as well, of course, but we are concerned with recent popularity. Because so many people have computers now, and regularly surf the net, all one has to do is type in the single word "haiku" in order to be inundated with enough reading material to keep occupied for many months if not years. The trick is for newcomers to determine which sites will offer the most knowledgeable information and the finest examples of haiku. Many poets who are new to the global haiku community will have preconceived ideas about haiku, most often learned from their grade-school teachers. The challenge for them is to be able to let go of what they've come to believe in order to discover what depths it is possible for the tool of haiku to plumb.

Another important cause of the burgeoning popularity of haiku in the U.S. can be traced to the efforts of a number of individuals for whom haiku holds a central position in their lives. Those few individuals tirelessly dedicate their time to giving workshops, founding journals or organizations, and then volunteering to be officers for those organizations or to edit the journals, and to organize events that promote haiku. The correspondence alone in such impassioned campaigns is usually very time-consuming. Organizations such as H.S.A., with all its regional groups, each with its own haiku-nurturing committee, and the Yuki Teikei Society of the U.S. and Canada, and most recently The Haiku Foundation, have fine-tuned their operations to more efficiently spread the word—why haiku merits serious consideration by those who recognize the need for poetry in their lives. Again, the most effective means has been the internet, but we should not downplay the value of special haiku events, and regular group meetings at the local level. There are also regularly scheduled annual and bi-annual conferences that always draw interested newcomers.

*Hsieh*: Could you explain the similarities and major differences between the English-language haiku and the Japanese haiku today?

*Herold*: Obviously, the two languages (as well as the two cultures) are very different. Just in terms of the outward form, the Japanese onji (sound-byte) is uniform in length whereas the English syllable can be very brief: "it," or drawn out: "scroll." Because of this we have come to see the traditional style English-language haiku as approximately three to five syllables shorter than the Japanese, on average. Of course, this is a broad generalization. Some poets favor a minimalist approach, often composing poems of fewer than ten syllables while poets who wish to follow a more traditional path, cleave to the Japanese example. A few still try to achieve a seventeen-syllable (5-7-5) arrangement. Add to this the difference in how a poem is cut. We use line-breaks or punctuation. The Japanese use kireji (cutting words, like "ya," or "keri," or "kana"). There are, to my knowledge, at least eighteen kireji in use.
From a cultural standpoint, there are also some big differences. Haiku hitched a ride to the U.S. on a wave of interest in Zen. Accordingly, a Zen perspective was considered by many early writers to be the essential approach to having a haiku experience. Later, of course, this led to a reaction against the rigid adherence to Zen principles. The Zen issue seems to have been contentious only in the

West. Most Japanese do not think of Zen when they think of haiku, or vise versa. The two are independent. That has been a big difference between cultures until the last decade or so. Now, there is a far higher percentage of U.S. haiku poets who have veered away from the Zen connection. And recently, our more avant-garde poets have become infatuated with gendai haiku. This new trajectory can be attributed largely to the groundbreaking book by Richard Gilbert, *Poems of Consciousness* (Red Moon Press, 2008), which describes a popular movement in modern Japanese haiku circles.

Another difference is that the Japanese aren't loath to use personification in their haiku. Although many Western poets still new to haiku also personify, more knowledgeable Westerners, (especially editors, society leaders, etc.) generally do try to put forward the idea that personification strays from the traditional haiku principle that we represent things just as they are, and avoid making overt comparisons. As for similarities, I believe there still are many. Using implication as a tool to guide readers to the essential emotional core of the poem is still an important feature on both sides of the pond. The images the poet provides imply his or her emotional state. By connecting the images, a reader recognizes what the poet is feeling and can relate to it from their own personal experience.

*Hsieh*: How has haiku influenced the mainstream poetry in the United States?

*Herold*: I don't believe it has had much influence at all. Even though poets of high standing in the mainstream, poets such as Billy Collins and Sam Hamill, Cid Corman, Diane DiPrima, Michael McClure, Steve Sanfield, Sonia Sanchez, and others have dabbled in haiku, that doesn't seem to have spread the popularity of haiku to other mainstream poets nearly as much as one might expect. Of course, in the early days of haiku in this country, poets like Jack Kerouac and Gary Snyder helped put haiku on the map, but their biggest influence was in the realm of Zen. Haiku came riding into the world of Western poetry on the back of Zen so to speak.

*Hsieh*: Could you talk about how you became so interested in haiku?

*Herold*: I first learned that haiku existed at Tassajara Monastery in California, back in 1968. I had actually written a haiku by accident, but didn't know it. I'd just been through a powerful experience, so I jotted down a note describing the images that precipitated it. Then I shared what I'd written with the head monk, Ed Brown. "Nice haiku," he said. I said, "Oh. What's that?" Over the next ten or eleven years I didn't write many haiku, probably no more than fifty. My interests were elsewhere. My interest was rekindled in 1980 when a publisher friend read the few poems I'd written and wanted to make a book of them. That got my juices flowing, so I wrote a hundred more. They weren't very good haiku by today's standards. Of course, I thought they were at the time and so I began to develop an addiction. I chanced to purchase a copy of *Zen Haiku and other Zen Poems* by J. W. Hackett and was deeply inspired by what I read. That book strongly influenced my own direction. As it turned out, Jim Hackett and I lived in the same rural town, just a few blocks from one another. We eventually became friends, and I even became his gardener for a while. Another mentor, David LeCount, also lived in our tiny town. Both men helped me immeasurably as I worked to better my craft. This ripening all took place during the 80s. I wrote a lot more haiku during those years, but it wasn't until 1990 that I learned that there was an actual haiku community in the United States, the Haiku Society of America. There was a regional group in San Francisco so I started to attend regular meetings. Through them I became aware of the resources available at that time. I also became familiar with many other poets who regularly wrote and published their haiku. From 1990 on, I was totally hooked and immersed myself in all things haiku.

*Hsieh*: You were once a student of the influential Zen master Shunryu Suzuki. How did you get into Zen and how has that experience helped shape the way you write haiku in English?

*Herold*: I discovered Zen (or perhaps it was the other way around) by way of my high school girlfriend's mother. She invited Suzuki, Roshi to come to her house once a week to lead meditation and to give dharma talks. She also tape-recorded all of those talks. The recordings eventually became the book, *Zen Mind, Beginner's Mind*. It was through exposure to Suzuki, Roshi at Marian Derby's home that I became interested in Zen. I was nineteen at the time. Marian lent me several books on Zen. It wasn't long before I began to sit with the group, at first in the Derby's living room but then we transformed their garage into a zendo. They named it "Haiku Zendo" because there was room enough for just seventeen cushions.

At the time, I didn't even know what a haiku was. A year later, with permission from Suzuki, Roshi, and Kobun Chino Otagawa, Roshi, I attended a training period at Tassajara Zen Mountain Center. It was there that I wrote my first haiku. I was twenty years old at the time—still very energetic and impatient. Because of this, Zen practice was very difficult, but it helped me to slow down, to be present, and thereby appreciate what was happening in and around me at any given moment. Haiku practice does the same. With haiku, however, there is the additional element of finding words to express what is perceived. When practicing Zen, it is hoped that the words that flow in will also be allowed to flow back out again, unimpeded by attachments.

One way Zen practice has informed my haiku-writing is that I've learned to appreciate things as they intrinsically are, rather than evaluating them or comparing them to other things. When I use words to compose a haiku, I want to point directly to the images that inspired me to write, to the poetic uniqueness of experience. Zen practice has also taught me to not be in a hurry. When applied to haiku, I find that my most effective work comes when I allow plenty of time for an experience to settle into my mind before I reach for paper and a pen. While thus contemplating, extraneous words fall away, leaving the words that best convey the experience. Only then will I write.

*Hsieh*: When you founded *The Heron's Nest*, what was your vision then?

*Herold*: It's the same now as it was back in the summer of 1998 when Alex Benedict and I decided to found the journal. We wanted to showcase haiku that we considered to be of the highest quality, poems that also skillfully combined the honoring of traditional values with modern means of communicating. I came up with the motto, "Where tradition and innovation meet and complement each other" because of a schism I perceived in the haiku community, one that had long disturbed me. Traditionalists adhered closely to Japanese conventions, often (in my opinion) too rigidly. If you consider a haiku moment (inspiration) to be a round peg, then too tight a grip on convention constitutes the square hole into which the poet then attempts to jam the peg. More often than not the result is awkward syntax that has lost the vitality of the inspiration. At the other end of the spectrum are the "modern" haiku poets, the innovators. It has always seemed to me that "the rules" were too easily being jettisoned by many of these poets in their attempts to artfully relate experiences. True, the results are often artful, but that is also the problem. The poet's skill becomes more important than the transmission of the experience. I think of the old adage about the jeweled finger pointing at the moon.

To my mind, the most effective approach is to blend respect for traditional values with the necessary innovation to breathe life into the expression of an inspired moment. In other words, to honor tradition but to hold it lightly so that the experience itself dictates what words are used and what form will best convey it. Here again is an example of how Zen practice has affected my approach to haiku—I practice a typically Buddhist "middle way."

Another way to describe my vision for *The Heron's Nest* is to quote something Shunryu Suzuki once said. He said, "If you put a snake into a bamboo tube it will soon find its true nature." The bamboo tube is tradition. The snake is an individual poet's experience. Putting the snake in the tube is like beginning with traditional tenets when we start to write a poem—we try to fit the experience (the snake) into a prescribed form. It probably won't be comfortable. When we feel the contrast between the confinement and our true nature, we squirm out of the tube with a better understanding of who we are and how best to express the inspired moment.

*Hsieh*: In the 70's and 80's you pursued a music career as a drummer and percussionist. Has that experience enriched your writing of haiku? If so, how?

*Herold*: There is music even in poetry as short as a haiku. I believe I have always had a natural feel for music, especially the rhythmic aspects, and because of this it seemed a career in music was inevitable. My feel for rhythm has carried over into the haiku I write. It is an aspect of the craft that is important to me and comes rather easily.
Imagine a band playing for a live dance. The dancers are enjoying themselves thoroughly. Then the drummer misses a beat. He quickly regains control and the song continues. So do the dancers, but they have, if only subliminally, lost some trust in the band. It is slightly less easy for them to surrender to and enjoy the music. Now imagine a haiku that has an awkward rhythm, or a sibilance or consonance that is grating to the ear: too many "s" sounds, a combination of words that are difficult to pronounce, or one of the lines is exceedingly long (too many syllables). When we read a haiku, the musical quality is the first thing we encounter. Flaws in the rhythm and/or the melody are like dropped beats at a dance. They cause distrust in readers, deterring them from staying with the poem long enough to understand and to enjoy it.

*Hsieh*: In your opinion, what constitute good poems in the haiku form?

*Herold*: I would have to say that I am most drawn to haiku that employ clear, concrete images. I like poems that aren't mere statements, and poems that don't overtly compare one thing to another, make value judgments, or personify other-than-human nature. The poet simply gives us the components, without explanation or artifice. It is our job as readers to connect the parts in order to discover the emotion that inspired the poet to write. Upon further study, we may well uncover the poet's skill somewhere beneath the surface. That, too, is wonderful. The best haiku call us from our minds back to our senses and to our hearts. They beckon to us from the present moment—the only moment in which there is life. I also prefer to find kigo (seasonal references) in haiku because they place me at a point in the overall cycle of birth, growth, maturity, decay, and death. Finding myself at particular ephemeral point, I simultaneously feel connected to the entire, ceaseless process that is shared by all sentient beings.

*Hsieh*: How do you get yourself prepared to capture the essence of moments in writing without losing them?

*Herold*: Ultimately, preparation is simply a commitment to becoming more aware. For me, meditation practice is at the core of this, but really meditation is something that is to be continued once we rise from our cushions. It is like a flashlight to point ahead of us as we move through our waking lives. To answer your question more directly, I must refer back to a previous answer. When I suddenly intuit a connection that calls for a haiku, I don't immediately go for pen and paper. I stay with the moment longer. I supplicate clarification. If I were to immediately write, it would be too easy to get attached to the words on the page. There are usually better words and better ways of arranging them. When I wait, the insignificant words fall away, leaving the ones that best encapsulate the moment. Only then do I begin to write.

Sometimes, however, I experience more than one insight. I may be hiking through the woods, or by a river, and come upon a rich vein of haiku moments. When that happens I do take out a pad and pen, but I don't write haiku; I take very brief notes, jotting down the images that triggered the experiences. Later, those notes bring me back to the time of the inspirations. I'll take them one at a time, lingering, digesting, and then writing.

In either case, the important thing is to not lose sight of the moment of inspiration by being impatient to write. And once I do begin to write, I find that it is just as important to not put the pen down too soon.

*Hsieh*: If haiku is meant to capture the essence of the moment, how would the draft editing process by the author interfere with or distort the original experience or inspiration?

*Herold*: The most important and often the most difficult thing, is to not lose touch with the original experience. As we practice writing haiku, we each acquire the tendency to adhere to a set of parameters that are consistently rewarding. However, the original experience often does not fit so well into those parameters. Nevertheless they are a good place to begin. Then, being careful to not lose sight of what inspired us, it will become apparent which of those parameters must be sacrificed in order to best covey the experience.

Writing haiku is almost always a matter of compromise, but it is most important to cleave to the moment of inspiration. I can't stress this enough. If we sacrifice the inspiration, an outwardly fine haiku may result, but it will be a tribute to a form, not an honoring of the insight. There are poets who have become formulaic, producing beautiful but empty shells. Poets who remain true to their original experiences, however, will often come up with poems that are more rough-hewn, but have plenty of marrow.

Another point to consider is that, over the years, as our haiku files expand, we can look back at our work as if it was a journal, which, in fact, it is. How good is a journal that sacrifices truth for an outward form that satisfies preconceived ideas about what is "good"?

*Hsieh*: As a poet and musician, can you comment on the musical aspect of haiku, particularly haiku in English?

*Herold*: I think I covered this in a previous question, but to reiterate, I feel that if we pay close attention to the musical quality of language and incorporate it in our writing, we are far more likely to attract and sustain the attention of readers. As with taste, and the use of spices in cooking, too little attention paid to sound quality will often result in a poem that is flat and unappealing; too much musicality, and the attention will be diverted from the poet's experience to the poet. Just the right amount of alliteration or onomatopoeia, or even rhyme, will enhance a poem, drawing the reader further in. And rhythm, of course, is very important. I've found that more than three beats (accented syllables) in any one line is almost always too much. In short, the amount of attention we pay to the musical qualities of haiku is subjective, a matter of taste. Once we begin to share our work with the world at large, we begin to discover to what degree our personal tastes are also palatable to the reading audience.

*Hsieh*: Could you name a few of the most influential contemporary English haiku poets in the U.S.?

*Herold*: I take it here that you mean poets who are still living and who still actively share their haiku through journals, contests, and readings. There are many poets I admire so it would be difficult to name only a few. I also know of a few poets whose work is among the very best, but who publish rarely and so exert little influence on the haiku community. So, of those poets whom I feel are masterful in their work, and who also have a significant impact on the English language haiku scene, I'll choose to name a few of my favorites: Carolyn Hall, Jim Kacian, John Stevenson, Francine Banwarth, Cor van den Heuvel, Ce Rosenow, Peter Yovu, Ruth Yarrow, Patricia Machmiller, Jerry Ball.

*Hsieh*: How do you see the English-language haiku in the U.S. will evolve in the future?

*Herold*: I really don't know. There are factors, certainly, that have bearing on the trajectory of English language haiku in the U.S.. Perhaps the most important is the accessibility to haiku on the web and in blogs. Anyone who has at least a passing interest in haiku can use a search-engine to find many sites in which haiku are featured, discussed, critiqued, reviewed, and garnished with other art forms. Many of those sites show little understanding of the depth of the form, but some do offer valuable insights and present haiku of high quality. Since the advent of the internet there has been a flood of new poets trying their hand at the form and who publish regularly online. More and more scholars are taking an interest, and even mainstream poets are begrudgingly casting sidelong glances at the haiku scene.
The upshot of the flash flood of new haiku poets, resources, and innovative directions, is that I believe the traditional underpinnings, both Japanese and American, that gave rise to the English language haiku movement are at risk of being lost. The Yuki Teikei Haiku Society based in San José, California, is one group (with members world-wide) that strives to promote traditional values so that there will continue to be a conduit to the most basic and profound gifts haiku has to offer. I know of no other English language groups who have taken this stance, but I hope there will be more. It is important to maintain a pathway to our roots that is easily accessible.

*Hsieh*: What is your advice to potential readers of English-language haiku?

*Herold*: Most often the haiku we read are in journals or anthologies, either in hardcopy or online. In either case, there are usually quite a few haiku presented in them. My recommendation is to read only a few haiku at a time, and to linger with each one quite a lot longer than one might if they were to read the whole collection. When one finds a poem that is exceptionally satisfying, it is good to go back to it and read it again, even more closely, asking oneself what makes that particular haiku so appealing?
I also recommend reading the translations and commentary of R. H. Blyth and Harold Henderson-Blyth in particular. Other rewarding treatises on haiku are Lee Gurga's *Haiku, A Poet's Guide*, and Bill Higginson's *The Haiku Handbook*. There are many other scholarly essays to be found, as well as a variety of translators' renditions of the Japanese haiku poets. I also recommend reading Cor van den Heuvel's *The Haiku Anthology*.
In short, I'd say the more haiku we read and the more discussions we can enter into concerning what is and what is not effective in the craft of writing haiku, the more we will appreciate and enjoy the form.

*Hsieh*: Any advice to those fledgling haiku writers in English?

*Herold*: It is very helpful to find a supportive group with whom to discuss your work, preferably in person. If no such group exists in your area, start one! Or peruse haiku forums online in which there are ongoing chats. I belonged to a private online group comprised mostly of editors. We share our work, with in-depth critiques, once a month - an excellent way to get feedback. You don't need a group filled with editors, however, to have a rewarding experience.

And, as I just mentioned, read lots of haiku from various sources. It's the best way to discover what sorts of things inspire your own writing and what sorts of things you'll wish to avoid.

# Joy Harjo

(Credit: Karen Kuehn)

Born in Tulsa, Oklahoma in 1951, Joy Harjo is a member of the Muscogee Tribe. She often incorporates Native American myths, values and rhythms, and feminist and social concerns into her writing. Her poetry collection *She Had Some Horses* was well regarded as a classic for feministic awakening.

Harjo has published fifteen poetry collections, and several books of non-fiction and children's literature and screen writing. She is also a musician and organized the band Poetic Justice that combined the poetry with a music involving elements of tribal music, jazz and rock. She has taught at several universities including the University of Colorado, the University of Arizona, the University of New Mexico and the University of Illinois at Urbana-Champaign.

Among many awards she received are the Wallace Stevens Award in Poetry and Nammy Native American Music Award.

The interview was conducted by emails with Ms. Joy Harjo's concluding email dated April 10, 2011.

*Philip Hsieh*: Do Native Americans view poetry quite differently from other ethnic groups?

*Joy Harjo*: Poetry is poetry. It is the song language of the soul. This is the same for any ethnic group. However, in indigenous cultures that I am familiar with, words are understood to literally have power. To write or sing poetry is to call into being the spirit of the poem. A poem therefore is to affect change, in weather, in process of any sort...in the heart. Like all poetry it is communication as well as exploration in the art of language. Many of my poems are written to transform a moment, or to praise or to acknowledge a person. A person could be the sun, a plant, a creature or an elemental process. I grew up believing that poetry was to be found in books, in print. It wasn't until after I began to question the presence or absence of contemporary poetry in my tribe, the Mvskoke people, that I came to understand that most of our poetry is not published in book form. Yes, we have some noted poets, including Alexander Posey, a journalist and poet who wrote at the turn of the last century. Most of our poetry is literally song language, and is sung in ceremonial and secular dances and events. I came to understand that poetry and music belong together. They ache to be together. And when you listen very closely, you come to realize that dance also belongs. You will not find them far apart from each other. I believe this is true of many cultures.

*Hsieh*: How do Native Americans view time and space differently?

*Harjo*: There really is no such thing as a "Native American". That term came about in the realm of academic discourse in the nineties. Of course, American Indian isn't exact either. We belong to distinct tribal groups and we are not the same in thought and being. We live in different geographical places. What unites us is our political relationship with the United States of America. We are also united in our understanding of a dynamic connection between ancestors, ourselves and descendants, and in our understanding of a dynamic relationship with this earth and the layers of reality that constitute knowing in this world.

I am the seventh generation from a beloved leader, Monahwee. He was one of the leaders of the largest indigenous uprising in the United States called the Red Stick War. We fought to stay in our homelands. He was one of the people who knew how to bend time. There are others in the tribe who know how to do this. He could move through time and arrive at a destination long before it was considered possible in linear time. In my tribe we understand time in a ceremonial manner. We consider the cycles of the sun, the moon and the seasons. This is actually a very large question and to answer correctly would involve others who are the people's astronomers and philosophers. I am a poet, musician and playwright. Of course, time and space are the materials I use!

*Hsieh*: Could you elaborate more on "the layers of reality that constitute knowing in this world", particularly around the word "knowing"?

*Harjo*: Every culture has a map of these layers of reality, some more elaborate than others. Poets, musicians and other artists maneuver with them, inside them and around in creative manners. When I use the word "knowing" I mean, understanding with a wisdom that is larger and deeper than logic.

*Hsieh*: How do Native Americans view the relationship between men and the nature?

*Harjo*: This again is an immense question. And again, it would depend on the tribal group, and there might be difference within those groups. My understanding is this, and I am speaking for myself and not for my tribe, that is, I have not been designated the official spokesperson on these matters, the earth is a person. This becomes clear when you leave the atmosphere of earth and stand, for instance, on the moon. You then see earth as a person, one person. Each country is like an organ. The waters are the blood. The lands, the body.

*Hsieh*: What do you consider the unique contributions of the Native American voices in American poetry?

*Harjo*: Indigenous voices have been basically disappeared from American literature, history, arts, science and so on. We are usually only allowed into the American consciousness when we are wearing our ceremonial dress, are dancing and are on horseback. I am working on a music project now called *We Were There When Jazz Was Invented* that proves that southeastern tribal nations music was crucial to the development of American music. There would be no blues, jazz or rock without our music.

*Hsieh*: Do you feel that many of the poems written by Native American poets today still carry the pains and sufferings of many generations before you?

*Harjo*: Consider any poetry. The poetry, the arts carry the spirit of a people. I imagine that would include the pain and suffering of generations before. It also carries the joy.

*Hsieh*: Who are some of the most significant figures in the history of Native American poetry?

*Harjo*: It would probably be best to go by tribal nation for the songwriters are the known poets. As for poetry published in books and recognized by what I call the "over culture"--the overarching culture that calls itself "America", some have made it through. The first poet who comes to mind is known primarily for his fiction, and that is the Pulitzer prize winning author of the Kiowa people, N. Scott Momaday. He is the first native to win such a national prize. Leslie Silko, the Laguna Pueblo writer is also a fine poet but she is known for her fiction. Several fit this category. I would add Louise Erdrich, Ojibway, and James Welch, the Blackfeet novelist.
As for poets who are known for poetry, there is Simon Ortiz, the Acoma Pueblo poet, Ofelia Zepeda, Tohano O'odham who often writes in her indigenous language, Luci Tapahonso, a Navajo poet, Linda Hogan, Chickasaw and Sherwin Bitsui is one of the youngest recognized poets. Another young poet from Alaska of the Inupiat people is the poet Joan Kane.

*Hsieh*: You said in a previous interview that when you wrote you were often guided by the voice of an old Creek Indian within you. Did that voice stay with you most of the time? Did that happen mostly in dreams?

*Harjo*: I believe that we as individual humans are not solely responsible for our gifts. They come through us from our ancestors and from other relationships we've cultivated throughout our complex lives. We add our spirit, our work, our energy to them and make art. Henry Marsey Harjo, my father's mother's father has often been close to me. He loved words. There are others who have been close to me. Sometimes they appear in dreams. Sometimes they appear.

*Hsieh*: How and when did you begin to combine poetry and music?

*Harjo*: I always heard music with the poetry. Often my poetry is rhythm driven. My first attempt to combine poetry and music was in the audio tape distributed in the mid-eighties called "Furious Light". This was before I began playing music, and asked some of the finest Denver musicians to perform on it. I began learning saxophone when I assembled my first band, Joy Harjo and Poetic Justice around 1992. I spoke poetry and performed saxophone. I was influenced by Linton Kwesi Johnson, the dub poet from Jamaica whom I saw perform in Amsterdam in the late seventies, and by the poet Jayne Cortez who had a smoking jazz band behind her. As my performance developed I began to sing on my second album of music, Native Joy for Real. Now I combine the poetry and music in theater and have been adding dance. My show "*We Were There When Jazz Was Invented*" included traditional Mvskoke dancing.

*Hsieh*: Who are some of the poets that have influenced you most?

*Harjo*: I have been influenced by many, many, many poets. Whatever you hear or read becomes part of a catalogue reel and you may be influenced in some slow or fast manner. I have been influenced profoundly by the spiritual song poetry of many nations, by the Rig Veda, by Song of Solomon in the Bible (though I am not a Christian), by Emily Dickinson, Amos Tutuola, Okot b'pitek of Uganda and his classic Song of Lawino. I have also been influenced by Li Po, Pablo Neruda, Adrienne Rich, Galway Kinnell, and many, many others. I have also been influenced by the poet of saxophone, John Coltrane.

*Hsieh*: Horses come up in many of your poems, even in the title of the anthology *She Had Some Horses*. Could you elaborate its significance?

*Harjo*: My ancestor Monahwee is the person to whom I trace the horse connection. And there are others before him. And as I wrote in the preface for the latest edition of *She Had Some Horses*:

> And there was the horse who came to see me once in the middle of a long drive north ... I perceived him first by an ancient and familiar smell. Then I was broken open by memory when he nudged me, in that space that is always around and through us, a space not defined or bound by linear time or perception. He brought the spirit of the collection of poems that was to become *She Had Some Horses*.

Later was my horse Casey. The last time I ever drank too much was in a "proletariat bar" in Krakow, Poland because I was happy to meet and play music with some Bolivian Indian musicians and a Hawaiian, and we were all so far from home. In the

grey of the early morning, when I was whirling around sick in my hotel room, my horse Casey came to me with a worried look. He was concerned because his last "owner" had died of complications from alcoholism. I assured him that this would not happen between us. And it didn't.
Horses, like the rest of us can transform and be transformed. A horse could be a streak of sunrise, a body of sand, a moment of ecstasy. A horse could be all of this at the same time. Or a horse might be nothing at all, but the imagination of the wind. Or a herd of horses galloping from one song to the next could become a book of poetry—

*Hsieh*: If everything can transform into everything else, why did horses become the "carrier" of this transcendental meditation process?

*Harjo*: This world we are in is predominately mystery. The space between molecules is many times more massive than the known universe. Who knows why each of us has particular obsessions, or is called toward a particular road? There are ancestral urgings, soul urgings, cultural and social streams. I don't know exactly why the horses chose me.
I was reminded by a musician/professor friend Barrett Martin that the Tohono O'odham people believe that songs are already constructed in this place of mystery. You have to pull them down.

*Hsieh*: It is said poetry is about memory. Do you echo that kind of thinking?

*Harjo*: Perhaps everything is about memory. The line I just typed is already memory. Poetry carries memory and moves like memory. Memory moves like water through the underground of human experience. Poetry emerges from this place.

*Hsieh*: Could you talk about some of your most satisfying poems?

*Harjo*: I don't really like to talk about my poetry. For me, the most satisfying poems are "Eagle Poem," "Perhaps the World Ends Here," "This Morning I Pray for My Enemies," "Equinox," "This is My Heart," "We Were There When Jazz Was Invented (the poem)," "For a Girl Becoming"--

*Hsieh*: What advices would you give to the beginners in poetry reading and writing?

*Harjo*: My advice is to develop the art of listening. Realize that you have many sets of ears. Perhaps every cell has ears.
And practice, practice, practice.
And feed the spirit of poetry, and give thanks to those who have gone before.

# Naomi Shihab Nye

(Credit: Chehalis Hegner)

Naomi Shahib Nye was born in St. Louis, Missouri in 1952 to an American mother and a Palestinian father. Her poems often show ordinary events, people and objects from new perspectives of Arab-Americans and Mexican Americans and are based on heritage, peace and the voices of people who live near her.

Nye has published ten poetry collections (including *Fuel* and *Transfer*), several novels and children's fictions as well as several translations. Among the honors she had received are four Pushcart Prizes, the Paterson Poetry Prize and the Jane Addams Children's Book Award.

In 2009, she was elected a Chancellor of the Academy of American Poets.

The interview was conducted by emails with Ms. Naomi Shihab Nye's concluding reply dated September 28, 2013.

*Philip Hsieh*: How do you maintain a warm and celebrating tone after you've witnessed the tragedies and sorrow in and about the Middle East?

*Naomi Shihab Nye*: First of all, thank you for your generous interest in knowing what I think about anything! This is very kind of you and I am honored to speak with you.
The Middle East has hosted an overwhelming array of sorrows and tragedies in recent years, true, but anyone who knows that world, wonderful in so many ways as well, imagines and remembers there are also so many modest, gentle people going about their daily movements and activities, trying to maintain hope, loving their own lives and one another – we can never let sorrowful headlines (which belong to all our countries) dominate precious reality. Children are in school. People are falling in love. Old men and women are staring at sunsets, feeling tenderness beyond measure for their own places. We cannot let the terrible headlines swallow all these realities. I was very touched recently to read that the American writer Dave Eggers, whom I much admire, said he thought that we (the United States) needed to apologize to Iraq for one hundred years. I agree.

*Hsieh*: You stated previously that "---to counteract negative images conveyed by blazing headlines, writers must steadily transmit simple stories closer to heart and more common to everyday life." Very well said. How can we keep our minds focused and not let the media get us off course?

*Nye*: Well, I think poetry and art can help us here the most. And music and memory…whenever I feel weighed down by the melodrama and tragedy of headlines, I know it's time to go read some more poems or stories. To write. To absorb art and music and cook some good food with old-country flavor. We can't let bad reports own our thoughts.

*Hsieh*: When I read your famous poem "Kindness" for the first time, I was very touched right from the beginning, "Before you know what kindness really is / you must lose things…" How did you come up with the magic lines like those?

*Nye*: They were given to me from the air. I never felt I wrote those lines. In a time of extreme trauma and panic, I sat down on a little park bench in Popoyan, Colombia, with a little notebook and a pencil, all I had left after a robbery, and those lines came through my pencil. I have always believed in listening to the air. Something was trying to help me.

*Hsieh*: It seems to me you always have great lines at the beginning or the end of a poem about very ordinary things. Take the poem "The traveling onion": "When I think how far the onion has traveled / just to enter my stew today. I could kneel and praise / all small forgotten miracles. / …" Were these the first lines you wrote down for the poem? Where was the source of inspiration for these lines?

*Nye*: Well, that is very kind of you to say. In the case of the onion poem, yes, I think those were definitely the first lines I wrote. I believe in writing regularly and freely and many times, when we do this, we are able to enter a poem with ease. We are led. What happens next is often harder!
I read a quotation in a cookbook about the onion's

travels through culinary history and – sat down with my own notebook while the soup was simmering and – those lines emerged! We should never get too far from our notebooks. I still love pencils and simple pencil sharpeners, by the way.

*Hsieh*: How do you maintain fresh eyes for ordinary things such as onions, buttonholes, pulleys, etc.?

*Nye*: I am a simple person. Small things still intrigue me.

*Hsieh*: You said politics is about people. How do you handle the tone of politics in your poems so that artistic ideals are preserved?

*Nye*: Harder to answer. I try to keep things human-sized, as the poet Edward Field once said, "Guard me from Poet's Head, that dread disease/where the words ring like gongs and meaning goes out the window…" I think about regular lives. I am not a politician standing on a pedestal.

*Hsieh*: You traveled a lot and had been called a "wandering poet." And you stated that poetry slows us down. How do you deal with the seeming ambiguity here? And how does travel affect your writing on the practical level?

*Nye*: It is possible to wander in a slow fashion anywhere! Most recently I was wandering in England, at the fabulous Ledbury Poetry Festival, a 10 day event with 95 presentations, then in the Lake District at Grasmere, where the poet William Wordsworth lived. I have become most fascinated by his sister Dorothy, her love for and devotion to her brother, how she took the notes for his poems… One thing I like about writing is how portable it is. You can write on a plane, in an airport, in a hotel. You don't need a grand piano.

*Hsieh*: Which poets gave you most inspirations?

*Nye*: This list is very long. As a child I loved Emily Dickinson, Robert Louis Stevenson, Langston Hughes, Rabindranath Tagore, Carl Sandburg, William Blake – many voices. Some of my favorite poets as an adult have been W.S. Merwin, William Stafford, Lucille Clifton, Shuntaro Tanikawa of Japan, Robin Robertson of Scotland, Jane Hirshfield whom you previously interviewed, Robert Bly – hundreds of poets. I am a voracious reader and I think anyone who loves poetry should be.

*Hsieh*: It appears that William Stafford had significant influences on you, based on your previous interviews. What do you like about his poetry and his approach to writing?

*Nye*: William Stafford had a devoted regularity about his writing practice, a willingness to revise, a very flexible listening ear – always tuned to lines which might emerge from conversation or dream or memory – and I simply love his poems with all my heart and being. They feed me, they have continued to feed me for more than 40 years. I urge everyone to read William Stafford wherever I go. I honor his devotion to nonviolence, his lifelong open-ended teaching practices, his modesty, his clarity.

*Hsieh*: You had two albums of music produced. Has your interest in music affected your poetry? If so, how?

*Nye*: Well, I love music but have not written any new songs in many years. It is something I would like to do again. My favorite songwriter/singer has been, for 40 years, Tom Waits.

*Hsieh*: You have done many poetry translations. Could you talk about the triumphs as well as the challenges you had faced when you did translations? Particularly around the issue of cultural differences?

*Nye*: I have only worked as a secondary translator on texts that were already presented in some sort of rough English version. It is more interesting to consider what is gained through translation (a world of new readers) than to focus on what is lost (idiomatic particularity, original music, etc.) I am proud that my first anthology, THIS SAME SKY, an international collection of poets from around the world, is still in print after 20 years. Translators are the unsung heroes of the poetry world and never get enough attention. Right now I am enjoying the fabulous book of letters exchanged between Tomas Transtromer and Robert Bly (*Airmail*, Graywolf Press, 2013, Minnesota) who translated each other's poems back and forth into Swedish and English…

*Hsieh*: You have published many books for young readers. How can we get more young readers become interested in poetry?

*Nye*: Expose them to poetry! Make poetry part of every day! Paper the walls with poems! Give them collections of poems which might entice them. Encourage them to keep notebooks! Offer poetry events of all kinds and encourage them to organize their own readings and presentations…so many ways!

*Hsieh*: Could you offer some advice for the fledgling poets?

*Nye*: I always say, Read, read, and read some more – write regularly – and find a way to share your work. And, I might add, don't expect someone else to do your homework for you. How our work gets out into the world is up to us. Don't plop it onto someone else's doorstep and say, Hello, can you get this published for me? The answer is, no. You have to find reasonable, simple, steady ways to share your own work with places that publish work similar to what you are writing. And don't get discouraged. Be kind to yourself.

# Rita Dove

(Credit: Fred Viebahn)

Born in Akron, Ohio in 1952, Rita Dove was the youngest person to be appointed Poet Laureate of the United States in 1993; she served for two terms. With more than twenty honorary doctorates she has also received numerous honors including the National Humanities Medal, the Pulitzer Prize for Poetry for her poetry collection *Thomas and Beulah* and the Heinz Award in the Arts and Humanities. She was elected a Chancellor of the Academy of American Poets in 2006 and is an advisory editor to many literary periodicals.

She is also an accomplished ballroom dancer and classical musician. The critics pointed out that for Dove, dance is an implicit parallel to poetry.

Dove has published nine poetry collections including *Selected Poems of Rita Dove* and several books of essays, drama and novels. She is Commonwealth Professor of English at the University of Virginia.

The interview was conducted by emails with Prof. Dove's concluding reply dated September 19, 2011.

*Philip Hsieh*: Let's start from the fact that you're an avid dancer. How do you view the interplay of poetry, song and dance?

*Rita Dove*: The Greeks understood that the three were intertwined; of the nine muses, three are assigned to poetry (Calliope for epic poetry, Erato for love poetry, and Euterpe for the elegy), two to song (Euterpe again, and Polyhymnia for hymns), and one, Terpsichore, to dance. Poetry and song share a muse, while the muses for epic poetry and dance are both depicted playing a type of lyre. In our era, sadly, these sisters have been separated.

*Hsieh*: How does the physical aspect of dancing inspire your poetry writing in any way, particularly in terms of the rhythm?

*Dove*: Poetry is already a kind of dance. There's the play of contemporary speech patterns against the bass-line of the iambic pentameter of Shakespeare – which yields a kind of syncopation, a rhythm under the melody. The expression is continually restrained by the limits of the page, the breath, the very architecture of language – just as dance is limited by the capabilities of the body, and by gravity. Ballroom dancing has reminded me that poetry has a physical component – that the length of a line, for instance, influences how slowly or quickly the reader breathes.

*Hsieh*: Could you use your poem "Bolero" or any other dance-related poem of yours as an example to make your points more specifically?

*Dove*: Of all the dance poems in my book *American Smooth*, "Bolero" is perhaps the closest in imitating the rhythm and physical patterns of the actual dance. The ballroom version of bolero consists of one long beat and two shorter ones; the long beat is represented by a sweeping step to the side, followed by two shorter steps. It's a very slow, sensual dance, because the two shorter steps cause the body to dip and the hips to sway. My poem emulates this rhythm by using one long line and two short lines for each stanza. As for the subject matter: Since the bolero is a dance of longing, what better American musical analogy could there be but the blues?

*Hsieh*: You were awarded the 1987 Pulitzer Prize in Poetry and became the youngest and a two-term Poet Laureate of the United States, among many honors. Having had the taste of success at such a young age, where do you see your specific goals in poetry or literature in the future?

*Dove*: I was so surprised by both of those – the Pulitzer Prize and the Poet Laureateship – that I didn't have time to think about the future. All I've ever wanted to do is steep myself in literature, to write the best poems I could. That goal has never changed. In a way, I think this early success, as you call it, was a lucky thing, since it showed me how unimportant such markers are in the grand scheme of everything. I want to write the best poems I can. I want to continue to stretch myself and explore other genres – write more novels, plays. I wish I had more time for those explorations.

*Hsieh*: From January 2000 to January 2002, you wrote a weekly column "The Poet's Choice" for the Washington Post. What was your vision then and what were your motivations to spend the time and effort every week for two years?

*Dove*: I always think of what William Carlos Williams wrote in his poem "Asphodel, that Greeny Flower":

> it is difficult
> to get news from poems
> yet men die miserably every day
> for lack
> of what is found there.

Writing "Poet's Choice" for two years was my way of addressing that lack; all I had to do was picture a poem nestled among all the news from the world (and a book review is, is some ways, just another report), and I was eager to write the next column.

*Hsieh*: How did you develop the love and gift for language over the years?

*Dove*: I was always in love with words. To me as a child, they were both sense and sound – music for the tongue and mind. Music was my other love, and so I collected words that sounded as good as their meanings – **ragamuffin, mucilage, prickly** – all the different musics one could get out of a mere twenty-six letters of our alphabet! **Ragamuffin** was as raggedy and scruffy as the beggar children it described; I loved how the word **mucilage** churned around in my mouth and how **prickly** stung the tongue. I would look at the books on the shelves in my father's study and nearly swoon at the thought of all those worlds, pressed between covers. When I was ten, I took down the fat two volumes of

Shakespeare's complete works; no one stopped me or told me this was difficult reading, so I went ahead and lost myself in the chilly castle of *MacBeth*, the gardens and courtyards of *Romeo and Juliet*. I've never lost that wonder.

*Hsieh*: Could you talk about the motivations for and the historical context of your famous poetry collection *Thomas and Beulah* which received the Pulitzer Prize in Poetry?

*Dove*: I was just entering my teens when my maternal grandfather died. My parents thought it would help my grandmother with the transition if I would spend weekends with her for a while, since I wasn't allowed to date yet. We had a grand old time, some of it in front of the television – I'd watch harness racing with her, she'd watch American bandstand with me, and on Saturday mornings we'd drink coffee for breakfast, then go grocery shopping with my aunt. She'd also talk about her life, and she told me stories from my grandfather's life before they'd met, stories he must have told her. I had never imagined my grandfather as anyone other than my grandfather – not this young man who fled the South on a riverboat, playing music along the way!
Years later, a cycle of six poems under the title "Mandolin" appeared in a literary journal, *The Ohio Review* – these were the first poems imagined from my grandfather's point of view as a young man. I had no idea they'd become the kernel of a larger project until I wrote "Dusting", a poem in which my grandmother seemed to be demanding equal time. Oh dear, I thought, this might turn into a book! I was daunted at the prospect of an entire book of poems about these two people I had only known in their last years, but luckily I was already knee-deep in their lives by then; the only escape was to write myself out the other end. So I dug in and wrote the poems that

would make up *Thomas and Beulah* – the story of a marriage told twice, from each partner's point of view. I would phone my mother every Saturday to talk, and she would talk about her childhood. "What do you want to know?" she asked, and I said, "I don't know – just talk." They were the most rewarding phone conversations of my life.

As I said earlier, however, I started *Thomas and Beulah* by writing single poems, not a book – and the entire story progressed poem by poem. I wanted to bring narrative back into the poetic discourse – the grandness that narrative implies, the sweep of time that's mostly missing in single lyric poems, which are rooted in discrete moments. On the other hand, narrative poems can easily get bogged down in prosy transitional phrasings. My solution: a series of lyric poems which, when placed one after another like beads on a necklace, reconstruct the sweep of time. In this way, two lives are revealed in small, intimate moments; their stories are spun out against the panorama of the Zeitgeist. Personal history, with a small "h", is their realm – a history that falls by the wayside when Grand History gets written. And yet every day we, each of us, live out our personal lives, our private existence within a small-h history – shouldn't that also be worth preserving?

*Hsieh*: Do you try to use poetry or literature to invite the general public to better understand the African American experiences?

*Dove*: When I was Poet Laureate, I received hundreds of letters from all sorts of people – not only professors and school teachers, but librarians and massage therapists, grandmothers and retired army colonels, doctors and corporate lawyers. I was astonished at the volume of mail, the ferocity of the love many of these correspondents harbored for poetry – although often the letters would begin: "I don't know much about poetry, but. . ." I began to realize that the fear of poetry – or rather, the feeling that poetry was mysterious and elite, that one wasn't able to understand it – was paralyzing its potential readership. People are hungry for some kind of communication other than the preprocessed sound bites of the mass media. By rendering into language our most private hopes and fears, a poem can make those fears less daunting and our dreams more palpable. Through poetry we experience empathy, a communion that can transverse centuries and continents. If a reader can relate to Dostoyevsky, there's no reason he or she can't understand the African-American experience. Again, fear is the culprit. Wherever I go, I try to break down those barriers – not by explaining my poems outright, which I consider insulting to the audience, but by showing that the poet before them is a living, breathing human being talking about life in detailed, nuanced language. If they can relate to me personally, it helps mitigate the general fear of poetry, and then, hopefully, they also discover empathy for the part of me that is African-American.

*Hsieh*: Did you have a mentor in poetry writing? Who have influenced your writing?

*Dove*: Many mentors – if by mentor you mean someone who either demonstrates by example, or teachers who pushed me when I needed it, then got out of the way – have informed my journey. My father, who stocked the house with books and read them. My mother, who quoted Lady MacBeth while slicing the roast for dinner ("Is this the dagger which I see before me . . .") My high school English teacher, who took me to a book signing where I met my first living, breathing poet, John Ciardi; my writing professors in college; my husband, who is a German novelist and a genius at detecting excess verbiage. My instructors in the cello when I was younger, and later in the viola da gamba, classical voice and in ballroom dance as well, for their insistence on discipline in the service of beauty underscored my own mantra.

*Hsieh*: Usually where and how do you conceive the ideas leading to your poems?

*Dove*: This is an impossible question to answer. I can never know when an idea will blossom into a poem, and those ideas can come from anywhere – ballroom dancing, cooking, walking down the street, driving cross-country, exploring foreign shores, reading the sewing instructions for a pleated skirt. A nonsense rhyme my daughter used to sing as a toddler has inspired a sequence of poems, which is still in progress. The impetus for my last book of poems, *Sonata Mulattica*, which is based on the true story of a mixed race violin prodigy who premiered Beethoven's Kreutzer Sonata, came from a very short scene in a movie about Beethoven.

*Hsieh*: Could you talk about your typical process of writing poems, if there is such a thing as a typical way?

*Dove*: I work with lots of fragments, and on different poems, for a long time before anything coheres. I can start with a line that I instinctively feel belongs in the middle of the poem, so I'll write it down in the middle of the page. Other lines may gather around that original, or I might skip to the beginning and write until I get stuck, at which point I'll turn to another collection of fragments and work on them until I reach a dead end there, and so on and so on. The process is like assembling a jigsaw puzzle, and in time – days, weeks, months – a workable draft of a poem will emerge, and then another, and another. Each draft, clipped to its fragments, is filed in a colored folder, so that instead of designating a poem by a title that might change or a theme that can limit the imagination, I'll start each writing day instinctually choosing a folder by its color. Then the polishing begins, which can take months as well. It's a nerve-wracking process, but I've found it's the best way for me to cultivate the subconscious connections; though I find myself writing in a kind of limbo for a long time, I frequently end up suddenly finishing three or four poems in the space of a few days.

*Hsieh*: How do you see the impact of digital technologies on poetry in America today?

*Dove*: Just as we could hardly imagine, thirty years ago, that something called the smart phone would revolutionize our means of interactive communication, it's still hard to qualify and quantify the impact digital technologies are asserting on poetry today and will impart in the future. Language is becoming more and more truncated; have you noticed how much faster speech has gotten in movie dialogue? This means that our sense of rhythm has sped up as well, and our patience for receiving information grown shorter. More importantly, thanks to so-called "social media" like Facebook and the staggering proliferation of blogs, our sense of privacy, of what constitutes intimacy, is changing. We relate details from our private lives into the entire world via cyberspace, yet bury the essential urgings – our deepest fears, our wildest hopes – beneath the incredible busyness of this cybernetic conveyance – take Twitter, for example.

*Hsieh*: How do you view the poetry slam? And its evolution into the future?

*Dove*: There can never be enough poetry, so the rise of the poetry slam phenomenon in the past couple of decades is exciting because it has brought so many young people into the realm of words and emotions. Having said that, however, although the concept of poetry as competition is an ancient one, what I object to in much of the poetry slam milieu in America is both the ferocity and regimentation of those competitions, which tend to follow the patterns of professional sports by organizing into regional teams and sponsoring tournaments. This encourages the participants to write poems that will score points rather than touch minds and souls. Too much is sacrificed for timing and speed – which means excess language, words that do one thing only (like marking time or thrilling through rhyme) with shallow dimensions.
Let me be even clearer: Many great artists were hugely unpopular in their day. A great poem can stir up troubling emotions that need to be processed over time in order to impress the poem's full power. Obviously, such a poem would fail miserably at a slam event, where immediate reaction is the only thing that counts. Slam poetry is mostly performance; it seeks the audience and tailors its expression to that end. That's more theater than poetry, and its proper venue is the stage, not the page. The page can go to the stage (though it may not "win"), but the stage can rarely go to the page.

*Hsieh*: Do you have any suggestions for the most inviting approach to poetry reading and writing?

*Dove*: Read the poem aloud, in a normal voice as if you were just talking to your best friend, or to yourself. Then stand up and read it again. Try different tonalities, read it softly, shout it out, deliver it like a speech, mutter under your breath. Each time should reveal something else about the poem. In this way you can overcome the fear of interpreting a poem, even while becoming familiar with its own music and language.

Writing poetry is a private activity with a public yearning; in the end, the poem written out of the soul's depths fulfills its destiny only if another human being is drawn into those depths and recognizes something of herself there. So it's important to hone the linguistic tools needed to sculpt the language in order to assure that what the poet poured into the poem is what the reader takes in. Read as much as possible, across genres and cultures; write as honestly as you can, with no assumptions. Forming a writers' circle is helpful – a group that shares its members' writings on a regular basis. After the first few polite gatherings, where everyone will be careful to praise the effort at first, discussion will gradually turn away from the surface material and focus on how to render that material powerful and make the author's intent clear. Technique will take over during those public meetings, leaving each writer the freedom to pursue her or his personal subject matter – and its emotional environment – in private.

*Hsieh*: Advice for fledgling poetry writers?

*Dove*: The same advice as in the previous answer, with this addition: Remember that you are not your poem. Writing a bad poem does not mean you are a bad person, or that what you've written about is phony, unimportant, or banal; all it means is that the way you've expressed it – the words and syntax, the images, the technique – didn't do the job right. When someone doesn't understand your poem, don't take offense; you might want to go back and mull over the text to see if you yourself might have suppressed misgivings. And if you find that it needs more work, concentrate on honing the language – a more powerful poem may emerge.

# Jane Hirshfield

(Credit: Nick Rosza)

Jane Hirshfield was born in New York City in 1953. She studied at the San Francisco Zen Center after receiving her B.A. from Princeton University in the school's first graduating class to include women.

Her Zen Buddhist practice and her knowledge of classical Japanese verse have significant influences on her several collections of poetry (including *After*, *Given Sugar, Give Salt* and *Come, Thief*), prose (including *Nine Gates: Entering the Mind of Poetry* and *The Heart of Haiku*) and translation work (including *Mirabai: Ecstatic Poems*). Her poems speak to the central issues of everyday life: impermanence, desire, nature, loss and beauty.

She advocates exchanges of visits by poets from different cultures. Poet Laureate of the United States Kay Ryan called her "an elegant ambassador for poetry in the greater world."

Her honors include The Poetry Center Book Award and Columbia University's Translation Center Award. Hirshfield was elected Chancellor of the Academy of American Poets in 2012.

The interview was conducted by emails with Ms. Hirshfield's reply email dated November 26, 2012.

*Philip Hsieh*: You have led a very varied life including farm working, monastic training in Zen, truck driving, cooking and teaching. How have these experiences influenced the contents and styles of your writing?

*Jane Hirshfield*: Each of these activities requires close attention, and teaches you to pay attention more closely. It might seem that time in a Zen monastery might do this more directly than some of the other things I've done, but I feel all these activities as one continuous study. If you forget the time when cooking, the stew will burn. Much worse will happen if you fail to pay attention when driving an 80,000 pound truck. My poems attempt to convey precise experiences, to be clear while at the same time preserving the deep mystery and unknowability of our lives. One side of that balancing point leads to pedantry and boredom, the other side to confusion. Only the quality of permeable awareness allows poems to say what cannot be said in any other way. Experimentation and fearlessness are also, I think, needed to write poetry. As a young woman, I wanted to taste the actual flavor of human life on this earth, and so I did many different things. In the monastery, I lived without electricity, without heat, a disciplined life that was very simple. I was exposed to light, dark, cold, heat, being and working with other people, as humans have lived for many thousands of years. I could hear mountain lions walk down the creek in summer just outside my wooden cabin; in winter, the rainy season, the creek itself was the roaring presence. We were fourteen steep mountain-road miles from the modern world. To live in such a way is, I feel, a great privilege, if it is chosen, and for a purpose. I wanted to know things as they are, and myself as I am, and to do that, non-distracted time is very helpful.

*Hsieh*: You seem to value freedom and solitude a lot when it comes to writing. Why are they so important?

*Hirshfield*: A poem wants to speak to what exists but also to expand what exists. For words to have any depth, any largeness, they must include not speaking, silence, and a limitlessness beyond and outside of words. Poems are language doing more than language can do. Solitude, for me, is the water in which the fish of new thought and feeling can swim.

*Hsieh*: Your books of poetry have received many awards. Could you give us an idea of how much effort you put in typically when you compose a poem or organize a book?

*Hirshfield*: It's very hard to weigh the making of poetry on the scale of "effort." It's a bit like being in love. Your whole heart, mind, and body are in love. You don't have to work at it, yet you are engaged with every atom of your being. Is this work? Is it not work? You do many things when you are in love, and when you write a poem. Everything you have done before goes into it also, the way a whole weather system, watershed, and planet go into any glass that is filled with water and drunk.

Putting a book together is different for me from writing a new poem. I write poems, one at a time, not books. To find an order, to find a title, that is work, and sometimes feels easy, sometimes feels almost impossible. What is a bit odd is that almost no one reads a book of poetry from first page to last, as you would read a novel. You pick it up, you look here, you look there. The only books of poems I read in order are the ones I already know I love, from reading more randomly first. Yet, I have to orchestrate an experience over a book's pages, as if it were read one page after another, in case someone else does read that way. It feels to me like a museum curator hanging paintings—you know people will move from one to another and have certain thoughts because of that, even though they look at each painting as an individual work, and may approach from one side or the other, or from across the room.

*Hsieh*: As an accomplished poetry translator, how do you come up with an "optimized" translation based on different considerations?

*Hirshfield*: I have always loved the Mexican poet Octavio Paz's description of this process: a translator tries to find "the same effect by different means." You need, in translating, to feel the original poem's powers and gestures and meanings, and come as close to that experience in the new language as you can. We all know, of course, that no two people ever experience exactly the same poem, even when reading exactly the same words. Even in your own life, as you change as a person, the same words take on different colors and fragrances and meanings. As a translator, though, you can only translate the poem that lives inside you, this moment, in your ears, your mind, your emotions, your pulses, as best you can. There is no "best" translation, only the one you come to for this moment, in this moment's language. In twenty-five or fifty years, readers will need a new translation, for that moment's ears and tongue.

*Hsieh*: Which poets had most influences on you as a poet? And have some of the classical Chinese poets been among your inspirations?

*Hirshfield*: I have been influenced so broadly I cannot begin to name the range—from the ancient Chinese poets to the ancient Greek and Roman poets, from the poets of medieval Spain and India and Japan to the poets of contemporary Poland and Scandinavia. Poems have taught me how to be a human being, how to feel this experience of human life both more fully and more broadly. To enter a new kind of poem is the same as hearing an instrument or bird you've never heard before: the world grows larger, the self grows larger. I cannot imagine who I would be or how I would feel without the poems I have read all my life. And this is continuous with many other things—language, mathematics, sculpture, the multiple knowledges of science. A newborn infant knows joy, hunger, love, comfort and discomfort, and perhaps wonder. Everything else we learn.

Among the Chinese poets who have been close to my heart are Li Po and Tu Fu, Wang Wei and Su T'ung Po, a half dozen others. A classical Chinese poet who seems to be better known to American and Japanese readers than he is in China is the Zen poet Han Shan. But at an early age, I bought many anthologies of Chinese poetry that included many poets, and I was probably as influenced by poems by poets I cannot now tell you the names of as by these most famous ones. Speaking your heart and mind through images and outer description, the powerful bone structure of Chinese poetry's parallel construction and statements—these affected me deeply. But equally, the ways of seeing and feeling the world that are in them changed my life, and through that, my poems.

*Hsieh*: Readers of your essays can sense a poetic flow from word to word and from line to line. How do you do that? Do you have to work hard to get them where you want them to be?

*Hirshfield*: I write both my poems and my essays not because I know something already, but because I am looking for something through its unfolding in words. Your left foot moves forward, your right foot moves forward, and they discover a path you had not known was there until you find it. Once the idea, view, feeling are found, then of course I will work to make the saying of it better—in revising, I look at every word, phrase, sentence, paragraph to see if it might be made better.

But what is "better"? Some mix perhaps of both clearer and more surprising. There is no point of saying anything in the realm of literature unless it has not been said or known quite that way before. The rest is "writing"—instructions for how to make bread or assemble a bookcase. Literature—art—is the part that is both true and new.

*Hsieh*: Could you elaborate on your motivation to write an essay book as successful as *Nine Gates: Entering the Mind of Poetry*?

*Hirshfield*: My essays are attempts to answer a few lifelong questions: What is a poem? What is a good poem? How is it done? But you cannot look at the nature of poetry and not find that what you are actually looking at is our larger human life. They are the same. And so my questions about good poetry are also questions about a fully lived, fully open life.

*Hsieh*: In the PBS film "The Buddha," you and W.S. Merwin were the two poets who were invited to make comments. Could you talk about your entry into Buddhism and Zen?

*Hirshfield*: When I was eight years old, the first book I bought for myself was a book of Japanese haiku. I lived in a city, I was a child, what did I see in those poems? Yet in retrospect, I can say I was choosing my future—haiku are a kind of poetry that reflects the Zen and Buddhist culture it emerged from. The poet Basho studied Buddhism, and carried both the Japanese and Chinese classics with him in a knapsack everywhere he walked. The poems in that book of haiku were perhaps a knapsack in which I rummaged, and found sandwiches and a thermos of tea that had the flavor of Buddhism in them. Later, I would read other things that had these views. But I came to Buddhism through literature first—not named "Buddhism" or "Zen," but infusing poems that spoke with the voice and eyes and ears of those traditions.

*Hsieh*: As a Zen practitioner and as a poet, how do you cultivate attentiveness?

*Hirshfield*: The only way to cultivate awareness is by cultivating awareness. This is true in zazen meditation, and it is true in writing and revising and reading poetry. You learn to pay attention by paying attention, and feeling yourself changed by doing that in ways that make you want to pay attention even more. At some point, there is a gyroscope inside you. It is not that I am always in a state of perfect awareness, in which I recognize my connection with all other beings, with rocks and stream and trees. But there is something in me that knows when I have lost that sense, when I have fallen into forgetfulness or sleepiness or the grip of ego. You feel it as clearly as if you were crossing a stream from rock to rock and suddenly find yourself knee-deep in cold water. And then—this is my own feeling about what Zen practice is—you might feel, "Oh, how wonderful this icy cold water is." Zen practice is not about never falling into the stream of human feeling, it is about knowing the water for what it is.

*Hsieh*: Could you describe how your involvement in haiku affects the way you write western poetry?

*Hirshfield*: Not only haiku, but the older form of tanka (31 syllables rather than haiku's 17), and the many Chinese poems of four lines or eight lines—each of these gave me a strong sense of the way enormous experience can be held in the fewest possible words. Not all my poems are very short—but some of them are, and those poems are my own way of writing, not in imitation of the Chinese and Japanese poems, but towards something I learned from reading them, an experience of a kind of poem I knew I found essential. The Japanese haiku master Basho once wrote a haiku that says: "Don't imitate me, don't be the second half of a cut melon." A much earlier Japanese poet, Kukai, wrote, "Do not imitate the old masters, seek what they sought." That is my relationship to the transformative powers of brief poems in the Chinese and Japanese traditions. I seek what they sought.

*Hsieh*: Any advice about poetry writing in general?

*Hirshfield*: A poem is a quantity and quality of existence that has found its way into human words. To write is a way to raise the ante of your own life, and know it more fully and deeply. My advice today (I say "today" because tomorrow I would probably say something different) should be taken with caution: all advice is abstract, general, and useless. Still, here is a little. To write good poems, first you must live in a way that will invite them. Think interesting thoughts. Feel fully. Make memorable music. Observe opulently. Allow exhilaration, exploration, the freedoms of a child at play. Ask more. Risk more. Read everything, but when writing, look for what only you yourself might say. Weigh your words on the scale of deep truth, but don't imprison them in the actual. Understand that poems have moral weight in this world, that they will change you and others, that they are consequential. And still, in writing first drafts, try anything, be permeable, throw open every door and window to every weather. It is my feeling that in the modern world, whatever direction the main attention of a culture goes, art turns in the other directions. A line of poetry that's been much quoted from my most recent book says, "Think assailable thoughts, or be lonely." Want to be soaked in the rain, cold in the snow, thirsty, hungry, to be wrong in the service of deeper rightness. Be what Gerard Manley Hopkins described, when writing of the awe of the beautiful: "spare, counter, and strange" and feel what he called "the dearest freshness deep down things." That intimacy, originality, intelligence, and state of wonder is where the poems will be found.

# Li-Young Lee

(Credit: Donna Lee)

Li-Young Lee was born in Jakarta, Indonesia in 1957. His maternal great-grandfather was the first president of the Republic of China. His father relocated the family to Indonesia, Hong Kong, Macau and Japan before settling in the United States in 1964.

Lee's father frequently read to him as a child the classical Chinese poems. His poems are noted for their use of silence. Gerald Stern commented Lee's poetry shows the large vision, the deep seriousness and the almost heroic ideal.

He is the author of four poetry collections including *Books of My Night, Rose* and *The City in Which I Love You* and had received such honors as the William Carlos Williams Award, Lamont Poetry Selection, and Lannan Literary Award. His memoir *The Winged Seed: A Remembrance* was awarded the American Book Award in 1995.

Lee has taught at several universities and devotes his full time now to writing. He now lives in Chicago with his wife and two sons.

The interview was conducted by telephone on July 29, 2010.

*Philip Hsieh*: Do you understand Chinese?

*Li-Young Lee*: I can speak a little, but forgot a lot. I can't read Chinese.

*Hsieh*: I understand that you knew the famous contemporary Chinese poet William Marr.

*Lee*: Yes. Could I ask you what year were you in Pittsburgh?

*Hsieh*: We moved to Pittsburgh in 1977 and left there in 1998.

*Lee*: What part of Pittsbugh?

*Hsieh*: I lived in Murrysville which was next to Monroeville. I worked for Alcoa in the small town called Alcoa Center which was very close to Vandergrift, PA where you and your parents used to live. How long did your family live in Vandergrift?

*Lee*: We lived there from 1969 to 1979.

*Hsieh*: How did your family decide to move to such a small town?

*Lee*: My father was a minister. The Presbyterian Church sent you where they wanted you to go.

*Hsieh*: There were large populations of Italian and Polish Americans in that town.

*Lee*: Right, but how did you know that?

*Hsieh*: Well, many of my colleagues lived in that town.

*Lee*: Where do you live now?

*Hsieh*: I live in San Ramon in the San Francisco Bay Area. I admire your poetry. I read your poetry including the most recent anthology *Behind My Eyes*, which has a CD with your readings recorded.

*Lee*: Thank you.

*Hsieh*: First of all, I was quite confused by different stories I read about your family history. What was your relationship with Yuan Shi-Kai, the first president of the Republic of China?

*Lee*: Yuan Shi-Kai was my great grandfather, the grandfather of my mother.

*Hsieh*: You moved to the U.S. when you were about seven. And before that your family moved around to different countries. How had that sense of transience influenced your sense of identity and the style of your poetry?

*Lee*: You know, it gave me a feeling of homelessness, no homes. The idea of home was very interesting to me.

*Hsieh*: Do you still feel that sense of homelessness now?

*Lee*: Now is better. It used to be very troubling to me. I felt very sad all the time. Recently, I can get home here. On earth I can be home. For many years, I kept wanting to go back to heaven, back to God because I felt earth wasn't my home. I couldn't find anywhere on earth that was my home. That made me a little depressed, made me wanting to go to heaven a lot. Maybe when I was younger, death was very welcome. I didn't know how to value my life maybe. I kept thinking if I were dead, I would go home.

*Hsieh*: Talking about death, I found love and death surface a lot in your poems. Could you talk about that?

*Lee*: I had this idea that when we talk, we have to breathe out. When we breathe in, we get filled with life. When we breathe out, our life leaves the body. All human speech is done on the outgoing breath. The ingoing breath, the inhale, is like the feeding breath. We feed on the air. But when we go out, dying breath. When we talk we use the dying breath. When we write poems, I think we give expressions to the dying breath. So the dying breath is the real subject of all poetry because when we say a poem, we use the dying breath. Something interesting is, when I use the dying breath, the more I say the more meaning there is, but less breath I have. If I take a very deep breath, and I start to talk completely out to where I'm out of breath, I have no more breath, but suddenly there is more meaning in the room between us. So these are opposite vectors: With more breath, there is silence, but no meaning. With less breath, you lose vitality you lose life but you gain meaning. That's a very melancholy thought to me. The more meaning there is, the less breath there is.

*Hsieh*: So it's sort of a form of dilemma.

*Lee*: Yes, it's a very sad dilemma. But like life, the more we live, the less life we have, but the meaning of our life gets revealed. When we write poetry, the dilemma is here conscious or unconscious.

*Hsieh*: Yes, I've already read something along that line although not as clear as today. From my own experience I could also understand what you meant.

*Lee*: Dying breath is our medium. Death is our medium. Dying is our medium. We said language is the medium, but really speech is our medium. Speech is born on the dying breath. Dying is our true medium. And I think love makes it bearable. So dying and love, it seems to me, are two tensions.

*Hsieh*: Your father used to recite classical Chinese poems to you when you were little. Is that true?

*Lee*: Yes.

*Hsieh*: How did that affect your love of words and poetry?

*Lee*: You know, when he recited those poems I would feel I experienced a very high form of sanity. Poetry in Tang Dynasty and Song Dynasty was ultimate sanity. So when I heard that, I really felt that wow there was this great sanity in the world. I felt like, when I looked around me, everybody else was insane. When I heard the poetry of Du Fu, Li Po and Li Qing-Zhao and all other poets, I experienced deep, deep true sanity. I felt as if poetry was ultimate sanity.

*Hsieh*: Although you didn't quite understand every word of it?

*Lee*: Correct. I loved the music. My father would explain to me what the poems were saying. I loved the music of the poems. I loved the images. And then when he told me what the poem meant, oh, it was even deeper. That's when I realized that was real sanity.

*Hsieh*: As you began to write poetry, how did you integrate all those feelings or impressions into your own poetry?

*Lee*: I wanted to write poetry that expressed or manifested true sanity. But I knew I had a lot of psychological issues. So I had to work on myself, practiced meditation and all this kind of stuffs. I was in a society. And society, you know, is not so sane sometimes. I wanted to get back to the sanity that was in the ancient Chinese poetry. I wanted it in my own poetry. I wanted to reach for that.

*Hsieh*: Now, specifically you just mentioned you loved the poetry of Li Po, Du Fu and Li Qing Zhao. Have you tried to use their metaphors or tried to imitate the atmosphere their poems created?

*Lee*: Yes, I tried, but I tried to do it in the context of my modern life. They relied on images. So I tried to use images a lot. There was a lot of missing homes, slight melancholy, a lot of solitude and the kind of cosmic vision that I tried to embody. Their poems seemed to me connected to something very large. The speaker in their poems was connected to a very deep reality. And I tried to do that in my poetry. They used images as opposed to statements. I tried to do that.

*Hsieh*: Some writer here in the U.S. commented that you used the language of poems to create an atmosphere of silence, an atmosphere that is reminiscent of classic Chinese poetry of Li Po and Du Fu. Can you describe how that is done? How did you use silence?

*Lee*: The images in ancient Chinese poetry have a lot of solitude around them, a lot of silence. I think there is something ….how should I say this?

*Hsieh*: Silence in terms of what is not said or in the musical sense?

*Lee*: I think in what is not said. What I love about the ancient Chinese poetry is that they said something, but what they didn't say sometimes is even bigger, even more. All the unsaid is very, very present. The experience of the presence of the unsaid feels like a very big silence.

*Hsieh*: I could sense that a lot in your poems. Your poetry has a hint of melancholy. And I wonder if your subtle way of expressing the silence is the reason your poems have the universal appeal.

*Lee*: I hope so. I hope so. Thank you.

*Hsieh*: How do you get the metaphors in your poems usually?

*Lee*: They just came to me. I waited a long time.

*Hsieh*: If you have some ideas or feel for a potential poem. Does it take you a very short time to put it in writing? Or sometimes it could take you years to get to the second line?

*Lee*: Sometimes, a whole poem takes two minutes. Some may take ten years. Very different.

*Hsieh*: I was hoping you would say most of your poems were done just like that.

*Lee*: (Laughing) May be half and half.

*Hsieh*: Well, that's pretty good. OK. Some of the metaphors used in your poems such as light, dews, fire and wind. Are they similar to those used by traditional Chinese poets? In some cosmic sense?

*Lee*: Yes, but you know, there were poets who write in English used those kinds of things too. What I shared with the poets in English and in Chinese is the mystical grasp. We try to understand the world mystically and try to see the invisible and the visible. There is the visible world. And there is the invisible world that I'm trying to understand and trying to see.

*Hsieh*: Near the end of your long poem "The City in Which I Love You," you wrote "the days of no days, my earth of no earth I reentered." Doesn't it sound like the famous Chinese poet Bai Ju Yi who had this line "It's flower or no flower. It's fog or no fog. Midnight it came and at dawn it left"? It seems you alternately used the real and the emptiness in the images. Is that emptiness sort of related to the silence in your poems?

*Lee*: Yes. I think so. But, you know, in that poem I really was feeling like we live on earth but are ruining the earth. There are two meanings: a philosophical feeling like Bai Ju Yi's "flowers or no flowers", but also a very concrete feeling.

*Hsieh*: I see, but what about the "days of no days"?

*Lee*: I felt as if life on earth is becoming…..Human beings would no longer have our days. Maybe someday soon human beings would not be around anymore. We just killed ourselves off. I think it's a very pessimistic thing to say. Concretely that's what it was, but philosophically it is emptiness and no emptiness and fullness and void. I tried to do both things, existentially and philosophically. Don't you feel that when we write poems, we try to say everything? I think the paradigm for poetry is DNA, that is, as much information in as little space as possible.

*Hsieh*: I like that metaphor of your using DNA for writing poetry. Your father was a monumental and, at the same time, a sensitive figure in your poems. Could there be a day when the presence of your father disappears in your poetry?

*Lee*: I don't know. Part of me hopes not and part of me hopes I can grow up and someday he won't be there. And then part of me hopes he will always be there. I think I'm a Chinese son. So my mother and my father are very important to me.

*Hsieh*: Yes, I can sense from your poems that your relationships with your parents were so strong.

*Lee*: My mother and father suffered a lot. I think when parents suffer so much, the children, consciously or unconsciously, try to take it on. That's what I had done.

*Hsieh*: Yes, I saw many new immigrants were like that.

*Lee*: Yes.

*Hsieh*: When and how did you become interested in writing poems in English?

*Lee*: When I started to learn English, I thought English was so interesting. I thought at first English was very funny. English has no tone. It is very monotonous. I used to imitate English. From the very start, I liked to play with English, rhyming English words. I remembered one time when I was very young. I told my mother a chattering bird was teaching me English. And I thought I knew English. She said, "Say something", I would just garble. I thought I was speaking English as a boy. I was fascinating with English.

*Hsieh*: That's funny. The U.S. Poet Laureate Kay Ryan was teaching at a community college in the Bay Area. In one of her talks, she mentioned she had many foreign students in the class. She was always amazed by the new way those foreign students used English words because they started fresh and found English to be quite interesting too.

*Lee*: Yeah.

*Hsieh*: In your poem "Eating Alone," you wrote "What more could I as a young man want"? How would you describe your life as a young man?

*Lee*: I don't want to be exaggerating too much. I think it was very lonely. Maybe a little troubled, but mostly lonely.

*Hsieh*: Now, would your parents be concerned with that then?

*Lee*: No, I think they were too distracted by their lives. There were a lot of things for them to pay attention to. Something like that they didn't notice it. But maybe that's good. Maybe that's where I found poetry. I think there is loneliness in ancient Chinese poetry. I love that loneliness. When my parents recited those poems and explained to me what they meant, I felt like "Oh, those were my brothers and sisters." I felt exactly that way.

*Hsieh*: Very interesting. Could you talk a little bit about your experience when you studied writing at Pitt? Later on I found out they had a fairly well known program on creative nonfiction. But I didn't realize it's actually bigger than that.

*Lee*: Yeah. They had a very good poetry program too. I had very good time there. I met very good teachers. You know, before I met the teachers at Pitt, I thought I was just some weird Chinese kid. First of all, I couldn't find anybody who liked poetry. I couldn't find any Chinese students who liked poetry. So I was completely alone. In my last year at Pitt as a senior, I found the poetry class.

*Hsieh*: That was taught by Gerald Stern?

*Lee*: Yes. He was so kind to me, so encouraging. Suddenly, I realized I was not so strange. There were people in the world who like poetry. So I started to discover poetry. That's when I discovered poetry in English.

*Hsieh*: So after that it's a journey of no return.

*Lee*: Yes. You're right. (Laughing)

*Hsieh*: Do you have any advice for young poets who are just making their first steps?

*Lee*: I don't have any advice. I wish I did. I don't know anything. I thought maybe by this age I would know something.

*Hsieh*: I think you are too modest.

*Lee*: No. I wish I were modest. I just feel as if every day was a struggle for me to write a poem. I still don't know what I'm doing. I'm still evolving.

*Hsieh*: But isn't that a good thing? To me that brings freshness to your creativity. You approach it as if you started with a clean sheet of paper.

*Lee*: That's right. Exactly. I think it's ultimately good. But my ego felt threatened. I'm fifty two. I should know something. I've been writing for over 30 years. It's good, but insulting to my ego.

*Hsieh*: Are you teaching in any way now?

*Lee*: No. I'm not teaching.

*Hsieh*: So you are full time writing poetry?

*Lee*: Yes.

*Hsieh*: That's very unusual for any poets in the U.S. Now, you expressed the view that part of the mission of poetry was to help build heaven on earth. Could you elaborate on that? I noticed that in your poem "Self Help for Fellow Refuges," you said "Kingdom of heaven is good, but heaven on earth is better." That's along the same line. Right?

*Lee*: Yes. You know, my feeling is, when a person practices poetry just like practicing yoga, Taichi and Gongfu, we are in touch with ultimate sanity. I think the more we are in touch with ultimate sanity, the more we can build heaven on earth. I love I-Ching as a book of philosophy, not for telling the future. The first hexagram is heaven. Creative, initiative, power, clarity. I love the hexagram that's earth and heaven in harmony. That's my idea of heaven. The more people write poetry, the more they do any kind of art, the more sane they become. The more sane people are, the better our society will be. Someday there will be heaven on earth. That's what I was thinking.

*Hsieh*: So what role does poetry play in your current life?

*Lee*: Oh, it's everything. I think it's my calling. I'm always on the job, always listening for poems. My soul, I feel, is like a radar dish, always turning to try to pick up poems.

*Hsieh*: So you read a lot by different poets. Who are your favorite poets?

*Lee*: Wow, I have a lot. You mentioned Bai Ju Yi. I loved him. Pablo Neruda. Federico Garcia Lorca, the Spanish poet. Emily Dickinson. Oh, Emily Dickinson is so good.

*Hsieh*: From what angle?

*Lee*: You know, she reminded me of the Chinese. On one hand, very simple, but then very deep, very very deep. Can I read you a poem by Emily Dickinson? This one is beautiful. I loved this one. It's so simple like a child, like a very wise child who wrote this poem.

(*Lee* reciting Emily Dickinson's poem from
*Complete Poems* by Emily Dickinson
(Little Brown; 1924))

Poem No. 126

The Brain - is wider than the Sky -
For - put them side by side -
The one the other will contain
With ease - and You - beside -

The Brain is deeper than the sea -
For - hold them - Blue to Blue -
The one the other will absorb -
As Sponges - Buckets - do -

The Brain is just the weight of God -
For - Heft them - Pound for Pound -
And they will differ - if they do -
As Syllable from Sound -

I love that.

*Hsieh*: Yeah. It has the clarity and yet you can dig into it.

*Lee*: Yes. Yes. I love "The brain is deeper than the sea. For, hold them, blue to blue." So the brain is blue. And the sea is blue. But the brain is blue, she said. That's the color of sadness. Something about the brain. The brain is naturally sad, maybe that's what she's saying, you know. Then she said the brain is just the weight of God, pound for pound. And I said, wow, only a very wise child could say that.

*Hsieh*: Yes. If you look at her background at that time, it seemed she had that feeling of modern times. It sounded like her imagination went wild. I was exposed to a few of her poems, but now I'm getting more curious about her.

*Lee*: Yes. I loved that poem. That's poem 126. She had no title.

*Hsieh*: Did you just memorize that?

*Lee*: I wrote it in a journal.

*Hsieh*: I see. Any other current poets you like?

*Lee*: Among the American poets, I loved Jack Gilbert, Philip Levine, Gerald Stern and Galway Kinnell. Among older poets, Cesar Vallejo from Peru and Rainer Rilke from Germany. Oh, Robert Duncan. I loved Robert Duncan.

*Hsieh*: But why?

*Lee*: I liked Duncan's music and expansiveness. I loved Allen Ginsberg. I also loved Robert Bly.

*Hsieh*: I remembered Robert Bly had very nice compliments of your poetry.

*Lee*: And you know who else I loved? William Stafford. He's dead now but he was very good. He's like a Chinese. He's very interesting. He told me he tried to think of himself as a Chinese poet.

*Hsieh*: What you just said is very nice for me as a person. I like to read more English poems that have Chinese flavor.

*Lee*: I think William Stafford's poems, you will find, had strong Chinese flavor. Robert Bly, especially his early poems, also had strong Chinese flavor. James Wright's poems were very influenced by Chinese poetry.

*Hsieh*: Interesting. In many of your poems such as "The Gift," you are so good at transforming the ordinary situations into emotional excitement. Do the emotional contents of ordinary scenarios come to you naturally or do you have to work hard to get the connections between the two?

*Lee*: My own experience is that when I had an experience like "The Gift," when my father was taking that splinter out of my hand, I was so full of love for him. I felt so much love, so much sadness, so much honor and so much respect for him. I was amazed at him. I could have just wept. But as a child, I always had these experiences so big in me that I didn't know what to do with them. When I grew up, the poem moved to my wife. When I was taking that splinter out of her hand, I was so moved by her, so moved by her pain, her trust of me. I was just so moved by the whole experience. I think what happened was that I was trying to remember: I have been here before. When? So when I wrote the poem, I think I might have written first about her, and then went into the memory. But when I looked at the poem, I thought: No. It needs to begin in memory. So I moved that stanza to the front. It worked better that way.

*Hsieh*: I'm glad that you shared that experience with us. It makes sense. It's easier for the readers to get the connection.

*Lee*: Yeah. But I think sometimes that's what happened to me. When I write a poem about an experience, the experience was like the ocean. I feel as if I tried to put the entire ocean into a cup. It's difficult. So much feeling that I'm trying to put in.

*Hsieh*: That's a good metaphor. Do you philosophize about life a lot?

*Lee*: Too much. I have to stop.

*Hsieh*: Are you always digging into the meanings of different things around you?

*Lee*: Always. Always. Constant. I wish I could stop. I need to stop. Like in that poem "Self Help for Fellow Refugees," I said "Thinking is good. But living is better." Sometimes the thinking gets in the way of my living. I'm just always thinking. I'm not living. It's a problem.

*Hsieh*: Speaking of that, do you mind if I ask you how your wife could keep up the pace with you?

*Lee*: (Laughing) My poor wife. My wife, I think, is a saint. Anybody who marries a poet is a saint. She is just so patient, so nurturing, so giving. Just long suffering. She believes in me. Sometimes she can be very strict, saying "You have to write something. Don't be so depressed." She wakes me up. She is just wonderful. I'm so grateful that God gave her to me.

*Hsieh*: I think you said it in your poems. You dedicated the anthologies to her. You used her in some of your poems. We could feel it as readers.

*Lee*: I'm glad.

*Hsieh*: You seemed to value the aesthetic awareness by saying it's the most complete form of awareness we have. How can we increase that awareness?

*Lee*: Through the practice of any art form. Poetry is very good because it uses language. In poetry you need to use both sides of the brain. Maybe in painting you don't need the left side, the language side. You could just use the right. In poetry you need both.

*Hsieh*: I absolutely agree. It's a very powerful statement.

*Lee*: Thank you.

*Hsieh*: In an interview by Poets and Writers, you indicated you used meditation to help you write. Could you be a little more specific?

*Lee*: In my brain, there is a lot of statics, a lot of concerns, things that are going through my head. When I meditate, I learn to let that all go. After I let that all go, I can start to sense the poem. The poem comes from the deepest place in the mind, the truest center of the mind. Sometimes the meditation helps me let everything else go.

*Hsieh*: That makes sense. How long have you been doing this, meditation?

*Lee*: Well, my father taught us.

*Hsieh*: Is it right? So you've been doing this for a long time.

*Lee*: Ever since I was very young.

*Hsieh*: Quite an interesting father.

*Lee*: He's very interesting. A very troubled man though.

*Hsieh*: In what respect?

*Lee*: You know. It wasn't easy for him being in the United States. I think he's very smart, maybe brilliant. He painted. He wrote poetry. He played musical instrument. He's very artistic. But because we came to this country, so he had to earn money. He had to become very practical. He became a very sad man.

*Hsieh*: So he spent all his time filling all the daily needs, leaving not much room for exploring his life.

*Lee*: Right. I think he's a very deeply sad man. As a child I knew unconsciously he's a very sad man.

*Hsieh*: I see. How does your typical day look like in terms of your work schedule?

*Lee*: My typical day? I don't have a typical day. Every day I try to write poems. My mother lives downstairs. So I visit her sometime every day. I give her massage every day. She's very old. There's a lot of pain in her body. So massage helps her. I get a lot out of that. I don't know if your Chinese family is different or the same. But, mother and child, not a lot of kissing and hugging. So I gave her massage. It gave me a chance to touch her.

*Hsieh*: I completely understand what you meant. Let me change the subject. Do you tend to complete your first draft in one sitting?

*Lee*: Sometimes. Sometimes many many tries to even get a first draft.

*Hsieh*: How about revisions?

*Lee*: Sometimes a lot of revisions, even years of revision. And then sometimes the poem just comes out. There it is. So it's different each time.

*Hsieh*: When do you know if a poem is done and ready to be sent out for publication?

*Lee*: Wow, I don't know. There is a wonderful French poet who said, "Poems are never done. They are just abandoned." You just get tired of them. They are done. Even if the poem may not be perfect, but you don't know what to do anymore.

*Hsieh*: I thought you were going to say to me that a poem is not done, will never be done in the sense that the readers will finish it off or take it and run with another version.

*Lee*: Oh, I like that. I like that. I'm going to steal that. (Laughing)

*Hsieh*: OK. That's the way I look at a poem. It's never quite finished. The reader can take it and run in a different route. And you don't have any control.

*Lee*: That's true. That's very true. I like that. That's deep thought. I'm going to think about that.

*Hsieh*: When you have something published along that line, let me know.

*Lee*: Oh, OK. (Laughing)

*Hsieh*: Do you have any writing plan for the next few years?

*Lee*: No. Every day I just try to write new poems.

*Hsieh*: Do you use a poetry notebook or something like that to jut down ideas?

*Lee*: I do, but not on a notebook. I write on napkins, envelopes and back of my hands, everywhere. I've written on my shoes before. At a time when I listened to somebody who gave a talk and I thought about something. There was nowhere to write, so I wrote on my shoes.

*Hsieh*: My God. This is the first time I heard someone did that! Now I want to thank you for your taking the time to do this interview.

*Lee*: Thank you so much.

# Index

## A
*A Coney Island of the Mind*, 15, 24
*After*, 158
*A Path in the Garden*, 108
*A Second Look*, 35
Academy of American Poets, 97, 136, 144, 159
Aesthetics, 55, 85, 104, 189
African American, 88, 151-152
Aging, 30
Ambiguity, 139
American Life in Poetry Project, 83
*American Smooth*, 148
*Americas – Book I*, 22
*Autumn Window*, 44

## B
Ball, Jerry, 34-43, 121
*Baseball Seasons*, 35
Beat Movement, 23, 24
*Behind My Eyes*, 174
*Between Heaven and Earth*, 44
*Bicycles: Love Poems*, 88, 92
Black Arts Movement, 88, 91
*Books of My Nights*, 170
Boundaries, 102
Buddhism, 37, 40, 116, 158, 165-166

## C
Chicano Movement, 101
Childhood, 21, 69-72, 76, 99
City Lights, 14, 17, 18-23
Civil rights, 91, 101
*Come, Thief*, 158
*Connecting the Dots*, 26

## D
Dance, 144, 147, 153
*Delights and Shadows*, 82
Dove, Rita, 144-157
Draft(s), 56, 94, 105, 190
Dream, 130

## F
Ferlinghetti, Lawrence, 14-24
Float on the words, 79
Form of poetry, 38, 74-75, 101
*Fuel*, 136

## G
Giovanni, Nikki, 88-95
*Given Sugar, Given Salt*, 158

## H
Haiku, 38, 42, 108-123, 165-167
*Half the World in Light*, 96
Harjo, Joy, 124-134
Herold, Christopher, 108-123
Herrera, Juan Felipe, 96-106
Hirshfield, Jane, 158-168
Hoffmann, Roald, 62-80
*Howl*, 14, 19

## I
Image, 76
Immigrant, 72, 100, 180
Indigenous, 102
*Inside Out*, 108

## K
Kooser, Ted, 82-87
Kumin, Maxine, 26-32, 74

## L

Language, 37, 39, 50, 53, 58, 69, 111, 154, 156, 177, 189
Latino literary, 100
Lee, Li-Young, 49, 170-192

## M

Marr, William, 44-60, 173
Meditation, 114, 133, 166, 189
Memory, 42, 70-71, 133, 138
*Memory Effects*, 62
Metaphor, 31, 37, 55, 76-77, 80, 86, 178-179
Mexican American, 136
*Mirabai: Ecstatic Poems,* 158
Mortality, 30
Muse, 30
Music, 40, 41, 116-117, 120, 124, 131, 138, 140, 144

## N

Native American, 127-130
Nature, 29, 76
*Nine Gates: Entering the Mind of Poetry*, 158, 165
*Notes on the Assemblage,* 96
Nye, Naomi Shihab, 136-142

## P

*Pictures of the Gone World*, 15
*Pieces of Eight – Haiku Offerings along the Eight-Fold Path*, 40
Poet Laureate of the U.S., 27, 82, 97, 105, 144, 148, 151, 158, 181
Poetry, Chinese, 40, 42, 50, 57, 106, 164, 167, 170, 176-179
*Poetry as Insurgent Art*, 15
Poetry reading, 40, 87, 156
Poetry slam, 94, 155

Poetry writing, 39, 41, 51, 57, 67, 73-75, 85, 87, 105, 118-119, 138-140, 152-153, 156, 161, 165, 167, 175, 177, 180-181, 183, 188, 192
Politics, 139
Pulitzer Prize, 26, 82, 144, 148, 150

**R**
Revise (Revision), 86, 94, 105, 191
Rhythm, 51, 86
*Rose*, 170

**S**
Science, 52, 66-68, 77-80
*Selected Poems of Maxine Kumin (1960 – 1990)*, 26
*Selected Poems of Rita Dove*, 145
*She Had Some Horses*, 124, 132
Silence, 177-178
*Soliton*, 62
*Sonata Mulattica*, 153
Spiritual Practice, 37
*Sure Signs*, 82

**T**
*Transfer*, 136
Translation, 56, 141, 158-159, 163
*The City in Which I Love You*, 170
*The Collected Poetry of Nikki Giovanni*, 88
*The Heart of Haiku*, 158
*The Poetry Home Repair Manual*, 82
*The Winged Seed: A Remembrance*, 170
*Thomas and Beulah*, 144, 150-151
The Poet's Choice Project, 149
*The Metamict State*, 62

**U**
*Up Country*, 26

## V
Valentine Poetry Project, 86

## W
*What Color is Caesar?*, 31
*World between Mirrors,* 35

## Y
Young reader, 40, 99, 141

## Z
Zen, 111-116, 158, 161, 165-166

EGW Publishing
(Since 1979)

www.ingramcontent.com/pod-product-compliance
Lightning Source LLC
Chambersburg PA
CBHW021155160426
43194CB00007B/757